Margot Fonteyn

Pocket BIOGRAPHIES

Series Editor C.S. Nicholls

Highly readable brief lives of those who have played a significant part in history, and whose contributions still influence contemporary culture.

Pocket **BIOGRAPHIES**

Margot Fonteyn

ALASTAIR MACAULAY

SUTTON PUBLISHING

First published in the United Kingdom in 1998 by
Sutton Publishing Limited · Phoenix Mill
Thrupp · Stroud · Gloucestershire · GL5 2BU

British Library Cataloguing in Publication Data

A catalogue record for this book is available from the
British Library

ISBN 0-7509-1579-X

Typeset in 13/18 pt Perpetua.
Typesetting and origination by
Sutton Publishing Limited.
Printed in Great Britain by
The Guernsey Press Company Limited,
Guernsey, Channel Islands.

For Louise Brody Poisay and
Joan Bonnor-Moris

CONTENTS

Acknowledgements ix

Chronology xi

1 'There was Only One Me' 1

2 'That Indefinable Quality of Poetry' 10

3 'A Marriage between Music and Dance' 21

4 Ballet under the Bombs 30

5 A Tale of Two Cities 41

6 The Apogee 52

7 'A Multiplicity of Interests' 62

8 'Just You Try' 73

9 No Farewell Performance 84

10 'I've Never Been So Happy' 93

Notes 104

Bibliography 109

ACKNOWLEDGEMENTS

I would particularly like to thank Robert Gottlieb and Gail Monahan for reading the manuscript and for invaluable guidance; and Julie Kavanagh for encouraging me to write this book. Christine Nicholls and Sarah Bragginton have been my editors, and I am indebted to them for their patience, advice and assistance.

My friends Judith Sharp, Mary Clarke and Meredith Daneman also read parts of the manuscript; and I have profited from their excellent suggestions. Robert Greskovic was generous in putting some of his personal archive quickly at my disposal.

Word of mouth is how much of the lore of the ballet world has been passed down. For this book, I have often drawn on conversations and interviews that I have had with people in the ballet world over the last twenty years. Although I had no notion of writing a Fonteyn biography when listening to most of these people, I nonetheless gratefully acknowledge now what I learnt then from the following:

Frederick Ashton, Darcey Bussell, Pauline Clayden, Arlene Croce, Merce Cunningham, Mary Clarke, Clement Crisp, Margaret Dale, Meredith Daneman, Paul Daneman, Ninette de Valois, Leslie Edwards, Richard Ellis, Julia Farron, Robert Gottlieb, Beryl Grey, Dale Harris, Julie Kavanagh, Patricia Mackenzie, Pamela May, Elizabeth Miller, Gail Monahan, Keith Money, John Percival, Phrosso Pfister, William Poole, Alfred Rodrigues, David Scrase, Ravenna Tucker, David Vaughan.

This book is dedicated, as a belated wedding present, to Louise Brody Poisay, with whom I watched some of Margot Fonteyn's later performances and in memory of many happy ballet conversations, and, as an eightieth birthday present, to Joan Bonnor-Moris, who first urged me to write about dance.

CHRONOLOGY

1919   **18 May.** Margaret Hookham born in Reigate, Surrey.

1934   **March.** Accepted by the Vic-Wells Ballet School.

May. Taken into the Vic-Wells Ballet.

September. Works with the choreographer, Frederick Ashton, for the first time.

1935   **26 November.** As Margot Fonteyn, she is the bride in Ashton's new ballet, *Le Baiser de la Fée*.

16 December. Dances Odette in the complete *Le Lac des Cygnes* (*Swan Lake*).

1936   Creates the roles of the Woman in Ball Dress in *Apparitions* (11 February) and the Flower-seller in *Nocturne* (10 November), both choreographed by Ashton.

1937   **19 January.** Dances her first Giselle.

21 December. Dances her first full-length Odette–Odile in *Le Lac des Cygnes* (*Swan Lake*).

1938   **27 January.** Creates a leading role in Ashton's *Horoscope*; Constant Lambert's score is dedicated to her.

1939   **2 February.** Dances Princess Aurora in the new Vic-Wells production of *The Sleeping Princess* (the full-length ballet later known as *The Sleeping Beauty*).

1946   **20 February.** In the Sadler's Wells Ballet's gala first performance as the resident ballet company of the Royal Opera House, Covent Garden, she dances Aurora in a new production of *The Sleeping Beauty*.

24 April. Creates the central role in Ashton's new *Symphonic Variations*.

1948 **22 May.** In Paris she gives guest performances with Roland Petit's Les Ballets de Paris and dances Agathe in his new *Les Demoiselles de la Nuit*.

1949 **9 October.** She and the Sadler's Wells Ballet make their American debut at the Metropolitan Opera House, New York, in *The Sleeping Beauty*.

1951 **5 April.** Dances Chloë in Ashton's new *Daphnis and Chloë*.

9 July. Dances the female Tiresias in Ashton's new *Tiresias*.

1952 **3 September.** Dances the title role in *Sylvia*, a new three-act ballet by Ashton.

1954 **5 July.** Becomes president of the Royal Academy of Dancing.

23 August. Dances the title role in a new production of *The Firebird*.

1955 **6 February.** Marries Roberto (Tito) de Arias, who becomes Panamanian Ambassador to Britain.

1956 **5 May.** Dances the leading role in Ashton's new ballet, *Birthday Offering*, which marks the twenty-fifth anniversary of the foundation of the Sadler's Wells Ballet, which is henceforth re-named the Royal Ballet.

1958 **27 October.** Dances the title role in Ashton's new three-act ballet, *Ondine*.

1959 **20 April.** Is arrested in Panama and deported for her involvement in an attempted revolution by Arias.

1961 Dances with the Royal Ballet in Leningrad (St Petersburg) and Moscow.

1962   **21 February.** Dances for the first time with Rudolf Nureyev, in *Giselle*.

3 November. Dances the heroine in Nureyev's new staging of the *pas de deux* from *Le Corsaire*.

1963   **12 March.** She and Nureyev dance the title roles in Ashton's new *Marguerite and Armand*.

27 November. Dances Nikiya in Nureyev's new production of the Kingdom of the Shades scene from *La Bayadère*.

1964   **8 June.** Arias is shot and paralyzed.

1965   **5 February.** She and Nureyev dance the title roles in the premiere of Kenneth MacMillan's three-act *Romeo and Juliet*.

1975   Publishes her *Autobiography*.

1979   **18 May.** The Royal Ballet gives a special performance at Covent Garden to celebrate her sixtieth birthday; she dances a new piece by Ashton, *Salut d'amour*.

23 June. Dances for the last time on pointe, in *Le Spectre de la Rose* with Nureyev in London.

November–December. BBC-TV screens her six-part series, *The Magic of Dance*.

1982   **30 June.** Assumes position as Chancellor of Durham University.

1984   Performs for the last times at the Metropolitan Opera House, New York, and the Royal Opera House, Covent Garden.

1989   **22 November.** Arias dies.

1990   **31 May.** Attends a gala performance of MacMillan's *Romeo and Juliet* to raise money for a trust fund in her name.

1991   **21 February.** Dies in Panama.

'THERE WAS ONLY ONE ME' 1919–34

There were many secrets Margot Fonteyn liked to keep from the world, but her original name and her age were never among them. She was born Margaret Hookham, on 18 May 1919, and throughout childhood was usually known as Peggy. In her *Autobiography* (1975), she was often ironic about her stage name. Of one particular ovation at Covent Garden, she writes: 'It was a strange, almost weird, feeling to realize that I, or Margot Fonteyn – or perhaps both – was – or were – the object of that flood-tide of emotion.'[1] In the 1960s, at the apex of her fame, she and the dancer Jane Landon were passing through passport control together; Landon's real surname was Leach. 'Hookham and Leach!' exclaimed Fonteyn. 'Sounds like a firm of solicitors.'[2]

The young dancer changed her name, first to Margot Fontes in 1934, then in 1935 to Margot Fonteyn. She chose Fontes simply because it was her mother's maiden name. When the Fontes family in Brazil objected – they did not want the name dragged into notoriety – she changed it, reluctantly, to Fonteyn, 'the next in the telephone book'. Some friends of Fonteyn's were still calling her Peggy during the Second World War. Even so, soon enough Peggy was 'Margot', not just to those who knew her, but even to fans who never met her.

The whole caterpillar-into-butterfly process of becoming a ballerina was later to fascinate Fonteyn. Her parents were Felix and Hilda Hookham. He was an English engineer of painstaking and precise temperament who, as a boy, had spent two years in Brazil; she was enthusiastic, impulsive and sensitive, daughter of a Brazilian father and an Irish mother. Their two children were Felix and Peggy. Peggy, born in Reigate, Surrey, was a serious, contemplative little girl, who inherited her mother's striking black hair and more striking black eyes. The warmth and radiance for which she became famous were seldom yet in evidence. So how did Peggy Hookham become Margot Fonteyn?

'That child needs deportment,' her father happened to remark soon after her fourth birthday.[3] Acting on this, Mrs Hookham found a suitable dance teacher, Grace Bosustow, just around the corner. Bosustow later recalled, 'We sat in the garden and Peggy picked daisies. To me she had the most perfect grace I have ever seen in an untrained child.'[3] Like many dance students of the day, Peggy learnt all kinds of dancing – ballroom, ballet, Greek, tap. For a long time ballet was not her favourite, and she remained an enthusiast for other dance forms throughout her life. Subsequently, Bosustow noticed Peggy practising in her mother's garden. 'She really practised, going over the same step over and over again, which was very unusual for so young a child.'[4] Bosustow once wrote of Fonteyn, 'From the first I thought she was a sweet little girl and very original. . . . Her manner was very grave and somehow remote.'[5]

Fonteyn, like all ballerinas, is often spoken of as the self-effacing and immaculate creation of other artists ('*sage, modeste et belle*', as Dr Coppélius says of his doll-daughter in Offenbach's *Les Contes d'Hoffmann*). But ballet is too exposing an art for a dancer to exhibit in it qualities that she does not herself possess. Yes, a ballerina takes from her teachers, her choreographers, her musicians, her partners, her colleagues; but what she keeps finding, through them, is herself, and what she discloses to her audience is her own essence. Thus with Fonteyn.

'It was really all there by the time I was six,' Fonteyn writes halfway through the first chapter of her *Autobiography*.[6] By the age of six, she explains, she had won a dance prize, had discovered the pleasures of the sea and travel, knew that she loved to laugh and to dress up, and had become acquainted with both devotion and coquetry. Also by the age of six, she was capable of extreme stubbornness (notably in clinging to a nursery diet to which she adhered until her late teens). She knew her own 'bulldog tenacity', her ability to laugh at herself, and the importance of good manners. Perhaps most important of all, she had been 'struck with the greatest revelation of all: that I was an individual person different from anyone else. There was only one me in the whole of the world. . . . That moment I count as the start of my conscious life.'[7]

Dancing soon became the chief way in which she expressed this sense of her own individuality.

Becoming a ballerina involves, first, self-discovery; then, self-revelation. Peggy had rare dance gifts. Her limbs flowed in beautifully calm lines from her torso; she also had a slender waist and mobile back, an expressive neck, dark eyes – and compelling grace. Above all, in dancing to music she found her element. Music is the current in which a ballerina swims; and, in all dance history, we know of no ballerina before Fonteyn who found such buoyant harmony amid her musical environment.

Peggy had an instinct for the beauty of dancing in general, and for the discipline of ballet in particular. Whatever the pleasures of the world outside, the ballet dancer must return each day, like a nun reciting her vows, to the fundamentals of her art: the turn-out of the body and its limbs, the five positions of the feet and of the arms, the pliés, the battements and much more. Go one day without taking class, and you notice the difference (so goes the dancers' motto); two days, and your colleagues notice; three days, and the public notices. While Peggy learned in the classroom that discipline is freedom, elsewhere she developed an intense need for privacy. Her lifelong gift for concentration would often involve blocking off from her mind subjects or memories that she did not want to consider.

In many cases, a ballerina is the child of a broken marriage; in some other cases, the marriage later breaks up under the strain of the mother's devotion to her child. With the Hookhams, the latter occurred. Peggy's mother was diligent, encouraging, firm, self-sacrificing, discreet. Nonetheless, the matriarchal tendency in the family proved so strong, the mother–daughter bond so potent, that the parents eventually separated; and brother Felix, who worked as a photographer, later adopted the name of Fonteyn.

In 1927–8, Mr Hookham's work took him to Shanghai, to become Chief Engineer of the British Cigarette Company. His wife and daughter accompanied him, while Felix, aged eleven, went to an English boarding-school. A visit that Peggy and her mother made to England in 1929 lasted ten months, and Mr Hookham rejoined them there for a period. During 1932, mother and daughter took another eight-month trip home.

The whole period interrupted Peggy's education severely. However, it encouraged her – and perhaps encouraged her mother more – to focus on the importance of ballet. On their 1932 trip to London, Peggy and Mrs Hookham watched Alicia Markova dancing with the Vic-Wells Ballet. 'That's what I want to do,' Peggy said to her mother after Markova's performance.[8] In Shanghai, Peggy studied with several Russian ballet teachers, notably, in 1932, with George Gontcharov, a Moscow-trained dancer. 'Directly I saw her I knew she had a *ballerina's* head,' Gontcharov said later. 'Her face – she was very attractive, with big dark eyes – seemed to talk to me. She held herself beautifully. She was somehow always *intent*, as though she had some idea that she knew what she was about.'[9]

In 1933 Mrs Hookham and her daughter decided to leave Shanghai for London, to pursue Peggy's ballet career. Her Shanghai headmistress warned her that she would regret abandoning her education so young – 'You will feel yourself an ignoramus among other people' – and advised her to read extensively, especially the classics.[10] How Mr Hookham felt about the departure of his wife and daughter is not a matter Fonteyn later discussed. He visited them in London in 1936, several times watching her perform. His next leave, due in 1940, was cancelled because of the war. He was then interned by the Japanese as an enemy alien. Fonteyn and her mother did not see him again until after VJ Day in 1945. After his return to England, the Hookhams chose to live apart. He attended Fonteyn's wedding, and, in tying up the threads at the end of her 1975 autobiography (he was still alive at the time of writing), she refers to him fondly. Mother and daughter lived together in London for many years, and the bond between them was tight.

Fonteyn is often held up as an exemplum of the British style of dancing, and some people talk of how free her dancing was from Russian influence before her partnership with Rudolf Nureyev. Not so. The international success of Russian ballet in the early twentieth century and the Russian revolution in 1917 had resulted in a diaspora of Russian ballet teachers and dancers across the world. In Shanghai, now in London and later in Paris, Fonteyn was indebted to numerous Russian teachers, as she always acknowledged. Princess Serafina Astafieva was among the most important of these. It was in Astafieva's classroom that Diaghilev had discovered the ballerina Alicia Markova, then aged fourteen. He had taken her at once into his company, and, since his death in 1929, when she was only nineteen, she had gradually been developing a career in London as a leading light of all the branches of young British ballet – the Ballet Rambert (or Ballet Club), the Camargo Society and the Vic-Wells Ballet. To be taught by Markova's teacher: this would be something. But would Astafieva accept Peggy as her pupil? She was reluctant; she was already mortally ill and employed much Russian gloom. 'You must accept my daughter,' said Mrs Hookham in desperation. 'I have brought her six thousand miles all the way from China to study with you.'[11] This impressive line of argument worked.

Astafieva, a handsome Russian émigrée, taught in the Pheasantry in the King's Road, Chelsea. She was – so Mrs Hookham later remarked – a genius in spotting why students had difficulty with certain steps and in suggesting the right adjustments to particular parts of the body that would make the movement easy. Apparent effortlessness was a virtue that characterized Markova's dancing; Fonteyn always felt that it was from Astafieva that she in turn acquired this too.

'THAT INDEFINABLE QUALITY OF POETRY'
1934–7

'There comes a point when you have to let your children go,' Mrs Hookham wrote in 1978. 'They will either make a success or a flop – but at this stage, it is their responsibility, not yours. I let Margot go the day she was accepted into the Vic-Wells Ballet Company.'[1] Although Peggy was happy studying with Astafieva and felt unready to move on, Mrs Hookham made the decision to take her to audition with the Vic-Wells School. Weeks after being accepted into the school, Peggy was asked, as an apprentice, to attend rehearsals for the Snowflakes scene of *Casse-Noisette*. Later in 1934, soon after her fifteenth birthday, she was taken into the company.

The story has often been told, with certain variations, of the morning when Ninette de Valois, director of the Vic-Wells Ballet, first spotted Peggy for the first time. 'Who is the little Chinese girl in the corner?', she whispered to her teaching assistant, Ursula Moreton. In those days, Peggy did indeed look oriental: she had a wide jaw, round face, jet-black hair, and, at that time, slightly sloping eyes. 'She's not Chinese, her name is Hookham,' Moreton whispered in reply, while giving the students instructions. De Valois: 'Where does she come from?' Moreton: 'Shanghai.' De Valois: 'I *said* she was Chinese.' [2] De Valois added, 'I think we may be just in time to save the child's feet.' Perhaps she did save them. Yet Fonteyn's feet were to remain the weakest part of her physical equipment. It is likely that, had the Vic-Wells been a longer-established company with a wider range of students to draw from, Peggy's feet would have held her back. It was her good fortune, as she often acknowledged, that she arrived when she did.

She profited not least by watching Alicia Markova: 'I never took my eyes from her when she danced.'[3] No example could have provided Peggy with better incentive, for Markova was an English girl who had become a Russian ballerina of world class. From the first, however, Fonteyn differed from Markova. Above all, Markova's technique was part of her mystique. Not

so Fonteyn's. Whereas nobody saw Markova take class
or knew how she retained her technique, Fonteyn,
even in her era of greatest glory, took class with the
company. Fonteyn also soon displayed a sunny
warmth, and a mobility of the back, that differed from
Markova's example. Robert Helpmann, who had
partnered Markova and who, during the late 1930s,
began to partner Fonteyn, encouraged her not to
imitate Markova's unspontaneous, 'Romantic' use of
the hands ('dead hands', he would protest).[4] This was
an invaluable piece of advice, for Fonteyn's seemingly
simpler, un-Russian, but always poetic use of the
hands, bringing her line to an unaffected climax,
became one of the crowning features of her classicism.

The year 1934 was a key one for both Markova
and the Vic-Wells, with Nicholas Sergueyev staging
three of the full-evening nineteenth-century classics
for de Valois's company – *Giselle*, *Casse-Noisette* (*The
Nutcracker*) and *Le Lac des Cygnes* (*Swan Lake*).
Markova danced the ballerina role in all three. Also
in 1934 the choreographer Frederick Ashton first
worked with Peggy. For Markova, his muse, he had
made, in 1933, *Les Rendezvous*. Now he made a
supplementary dance for it, for four girls; Peggy
was one of them. The revised ballet was given on

3 October, the opening night of the 1934–5 season, and the fifteen-year-old dancer appeared under her new stage name of Margot Fontes. On the same night, she made an impression in the solo mime role of Young Treginnis in de Valois's ghost-story ballet, *The Haunted Ballroom*. From that point, de Valois in particular was convinced of her great talent.

Convincing others, however, took time. Early in 1935, when Markova indicated to Ashton that she now felt herself above dancing in some of his ensemble ballets, Fonteyn was the first Vic-Wells dancer to profit. In March, Ashton revived for the Vic-Wells *Rio Grande – A Day in a Southern Port*, to a jazz-flavoured score by Constant Lambert. The scenario, also by Lambert, depicted the seamy side of life in a tropical seaport. The Creole Girl was Fonteyn's first important part. It suited her youth, her warmth, her Latin blood, her plasticity. (She now employed her revised name for the first time.) William Chappell, who had partnered Markova in the original 1931 production and who was now Fonteyn's first partner, wrote that 'She proved to be ideal casting. Markova had not been.'[5] The fact that her role was danced without pointework, in heeled shoes, added to her pleasure. With this production, Lambert fell under Fonteyn's spell. A brilliant and inspiring man, who had conducted the first Vic-Wells performance and who was an invaluable artistic advisor and collaborator to both de Valois and Ashton (he had become the Vic-Wells Ballet's musical director), he now wrote to Ashton about Fonteyn and 'that indefinable quality of poetry in her work'.[6]

Markova now announced that she would leave the company later that year. Fonteyn wrote that summer to a friend: 'I cannot think what will happen next season without her; we shall all have to work very hard, but even hard work can't make a Prima Ballerina if there isn't one.'[7] De Valois began to share leading roles between Pearl Argyle, the guest dancer Ruth French, and five very young women: Mary Honer, Elizabeth Miller, June Brae, Pamela May and (the youngest by two years) Fonteyn. Ashton – still unconvinced about Fonteyn's aptitude for ballerina roles – first tried grooming her in other parts he had made for Markova. Next, he created a new role for her, as one of the two heroines of his version of *Le Baiser de la Fée*, his first Stravinsky ballet. He consulted the ballerina Tamara Karsavina, who told him she found Fonteyn 'very gifted and exceptionally musical' but that she lacked any understanding of *épaulement*. *Epaulement* in ballet involves the rotation of the upper torso on the vertical axis of the spine, the counter-rotation of the head, and the way that the eyes counterpoint the torso. 'From tomorrow,' Ashton replied, 'I will ensure that she does.'[8] The particular style of *épaulement* that Fonteyn was to develop – although less luxuriously textured than with the finest Russian ballerinas and with such later British ballerinas as Lynn Seymour and Antoinette Sibley – was beautifully eloquent, above all in the poetic address of her eyes to focus ideally her every movement and position.

Baiser had its premiere in November 1935; Fonteyn was sixteen. Ashton had learnt from Pavlova that a *pas de deux* should be a metaphor for love; Fonteyn discovered, here, in the *pas de deux* that he made on her and Harold Turner, both the wealth of Ashton's talent in this vein of choreography and also her own delight in dancing with a partner. Hitherto Ashton had found her severely limited and obstinate.

> I felt a great frustration in being unable to mould her precisely as I wanted. Her performance needed to be much more precise. I got very cross with her at times and went on and on at her, relentlessly. One morning after I had been particularly severe, she suddenly rushed and threw her arms around my neck and burst

into floods of tears. I knew then that I had won the battle; that I would be able to work with her. From that moment on we were never at real loggerheads again.[9]

Ashton's next ballet, *Apparitions*, new in February 1936, was to a scenario that Lambert had conceived with the young ballerina in mind, and to Liszt music that he had arranged. As a Woman in Ball Dress, Fonteyn was the elusive *bien-aimée* of high Romanticism, luring the Poet (Robert Helpmann) in various dreamlike scenes. The role had glamour, contrast, elegance; and Fonteyn's embodiment of the Romanticism in which Lambert had so steeped himself deepened his attraction for her into love.

The seasons of 1935–6 and 1936–7 were crucial for the Vic-Wells Ballet, and for Fonteyn. The performance that first won her recognition as a classical ballerina – and in a role in which Markova had excelled – took place on 17 December 1935. De Valois revived the full-length *Le Lac des cygnes* (*Swan Lake*); Fonteyn danced the role of the swan-queen Odette. Since the standard version of the ballet had been first produced by the choreographers Marius Petipa and Lev Ivanov in St Petersburg in 1895, Odette and her beguiling double, Odile, had usually been danced by the same ballerina.

Nonetheless, the second act had often been presented by itself, and thus several ballerinas had already been seen only as Odette. Fonteyn – who did not yet have the technique to tackle the bravura of Odile (that role was danced by Ruth French) – won all the attention with her account of Odette in Acts Two and Four. She revealed, in pure dance terms, Odette's dual yearning – a yearning on the one hand for freedom from swan form and for adult love, and on the other for seclusion, even in the arms of a man. Her amalgam of severity and vulnerability was arresting. The very purity of her dancing helped her to make Odette's plight a metaphor for a woman's mixed feelings about virginity: longing at once to break through into an altered, liberated existence and to keep herself inviolate.

In the summer of 1936 Mrs Hookham took her daughter to Paris, to study with the three great émigré Russian ballerinas, Olga Preobrajenska, Mathilde Kschessinskaya and Lubov Egorova. These former luminaries of the Imperial Ballet in St Petersburg were at this time probably the most renowned ballet teachers in the world. Characteristically, Mrs Hookham invited other Vic-Wells dancers to accompany them. The British dancers learned how to present themselves to (and how to charm) an audience, how to fill adagio dances with feeling, how to dance with Russian expansiveness and ardour, and how to master *fouetté* turns. It was a successful trip, the first of several.

The 1936–7 London season was to contain numerous further debuts for the seventeen-year-old Fonteyn. Three of these were in highly successful new ballets by Ashton: *Nocturne*, *Les Patineurs* and *A Wedding Bouquet*. *Nocturne*, a view of Paris to music by Delius, was particularly important for Fonteyn. She played a Flower Girl who is cast aside by a Young Man (Helpmann) in favour of a Rich Girl (Brae). Fonteyn's fragility here and, as always, her sincerity had an immense effect on audiences. 'I lived the story through at each performance.'[10]

Most important of all, in January 1937 Fonteyn danced, for the first time, Markova's two greatest roles: the Sugar Plum Fairy in *Casse-Noisette* and, most crucially, Giselle. The Sugar Plum Fairy was a role that Fonteyn danced with distinction, in Britain and abroad, up to the late 1950s; but it has never been part of her legend, as it is still part of Markova's. Giselle, however, was a role she danced frequently until 1970, and for many observers she remains the nearest they have seen to a definitive Giselle. Yet she herself expressed doubts about her achievement in the role: a modesty odd in the light of the tenacity with which she kept dancing it. What we can say is that, of the roles central to her repertory, Giselle is the role whose interpretation she revised the most; but also that her interpretation satisfied so many people that it permanently shaped their conception of the ballet.

As a girl, Fonteyn already had the ability to make audiences cry, or want to cry. In her responsiveness to her stage colleagues, she was an exemplary member of an ensemble. She was not one of the startling actresses of ballet; she did not alter drastically from this role to that. However, she certainly conceived her roles like an actress, working for deep-felt characterization, for dramatic coherence, for emotional truth, for spontaneity. While on stage, she had complete belief not only in her role but also in the stage world around her: 'I know Giselle very well; her friends; where she lives, the trees with the sun shining through the branches.'[11] She stripped Giselle of the genteel refinement of spirit that, in Markova's account of Act One, struck several observers as precious. Fragments of film of a 1937 Giselle performance show her heartbreaking warmth and simplicity, the extraordinarily affecting nature of her stage presence, and the physical elation with which she makes jumps seem to have more 'lift' than they do. Despite some technical shortcomings, the young Fonteyn's mixture of grace and innocent exuberance still has the immediacy of 'real dancing', as several other old clips of ballet do not; and her freshness of manner as Giselle has in no way dated.

For Fonteyn's Giselle debut, de Valois sent her a telegram: 'And some have greatness thrust upon them. Good luck. De Valois.'[12] In thanking de Valois later, Fonteyn had to admit that she did not know the rest of the quotation, or its source (the letter to Malvolio in *Twelfth Night*: 'Some are born great, some achieve greatness . . .'). Fonteyn now set about reading the classics that her Shanghai headmistress had recommended. Admirers had started to appear in her life – and she now found herself most interested in those who could lend her the best books or records. Once, on the bus to Sadler's Wells, de Valois asked her what she was reading. The book was James Joyce's *Ulysses*, a banned book in Britain at that time. 'For God's sake, child,' de Valois exclaimed, 'Don't read that in public, you could be arrested!'

THREE

'A MARRIAGE BETWEEN MUSIC AND DANCE'

1937–9

Fonteyn was a good storyteller, and one believes her when she tells of how she fell in love with her future husband in May 1937. And yet her account is not the whole truth. It is true, as she often recounted, that she met Tito (Roberto) de Arias in May 1937 while he was an undergraduate at Cambridge when the Vic-Wells Ballet was dancing there. She was just eighteen. The company danced on the tiny stage of the Cambridge Arts Theatre in the May Weeks of 1937, 1938 and 1939, and the dancers were entertained by the undergraduates 'in an almost continuous floating party, which moved from one location to another but never seemed to

quite die down for the whole week'.[1] June Brae,
Pamela May and Fonteyn – who were now such
close friends that they were known as 'the triptych'
– all met their future husbands among these
undergraduates. One night in 1937, Fonteyn came
back to the flat they were sharing to find a party in
progress. She heard, for the first time, a rumba, a
Latin American dance then virtually unknown in
Britain or New York. 'The music invaded my mind.'[2]
Two young men were dancing to it; she found that
she seldom took her eyes off the younger one. Next
morning, stepping out of bed, she found that her
feet did not seem to touch the ground: 'so I
returned and sat on the edge of the bed to think the
matter out. . . . The phrase "walking on air" came to
my mind, and suddenly I remembered the dark-
haired boy dancing the rumba the night before.'
(The sequence is compelling. She feels herself in a
new psychosomatic condition. Next, she analyses
the emotion. Then, only then, does she identify its
cause.)

She found that he and the other rumba dancer
were the sons of the President of Panama. During
the week, their romance developed, and he became
friends with many of the dancers. In the weeks that

followed, however, she waited in vain to hear from him: 'How the young heart can suffer! Perhaps in later years pain is deeper, because it has more knowledge to relate to, but innocence is utterly vulnerable.'[3] They spent time together again when the ballet came to Cambridge in 1938 and 1939; also in 1938 in Paris, when she was studying there. By then, however, her heart had hardened just enough to hide her unchanged feelings and her absorption in her chosen career had deepened. There followed the war, his marriage to another woman, and Fonteyn's ascent to world fame. Fonteyn and Arias only met again in 1953.

Let us believe all this – it is a wonderful story – but let us consider also a few other facts. Constant Lambert's infatuation with Fonteyn had become unstoppable by August 1937. He left his wife then, and soon initiated divorce proceedings. His union with Fonteyn had been physically consummated, probably in July that year. The rich Alice von Hofmannsthal lent Lambert the gate cottage of her London mansion at Hanover Lodge as a 'love nest' for his rendezvous with Fonteyn, and in August his wife Flo discovered.[4] Fonteyn's affair with Lambert, though known to few people outside the ballet company, lasted throughout the war years; it was both deep and passionate. Lambert worshipped the kind of classical/Romantic perfection that Fonteyn was coming to exemplify more and more. Her intense mixture of reserve and feeling, her at once vulnerable and unattainable persona, excited him. Lambert was brilliantly articulate; to Fonteyn, part of his appeal lay in what she learnt from him. She was by no means the only dancer whom he helped to educate – in music, in the visual arts, in literature – but it was thanks to him that she became far better read than most dancers, or than most people suspected. (Her 'Desert Island Book' was Marguerite Yourcenar's *Memoirs of Hadrian*. In her *Autobiography* she quotes from Henry Miller and Karen Blixen. In 1954 she read Samuel Beckett's new *Waiting for Godot* at the impresario Donald Albery's behest, and encouraged him to stage its first British production.) Was it Lambert who had lent her *Ulysses*? Certainly she read Proust on his encouragement.

Their relationship, however, was also ardently sexual. Not that Fonteyn's and Lambert's public guessed; around the theatre, Fonteyn always maintained discreet formality with him. Her home was still with her mother, whose degree of complicity in the affair is impossible now to fathom. Lambert had a son, and Fonteyn wished neither to seem, nor to be, a home-wrecker. But the degree of secrecy which she preserved around her relationship with Lambert is telling. And it casts light on the unshakeably discreet front that she presented to the world.

Part of what enthralled Lambert to her was her musicality. She could neither play an instrument nor read a score, but she had a profound sense of colour, rhythm and phrasing. (She later remarked that she did not regard herself as musical but as rhythmical.)[5] In later years, both Lambert and Ashton would remark, in wonder, how Fonteyn could seem to linger in one part of the stage when they knew that the music demanded that she would have to be elsewhere the next moment, and yet she always arrived where she had to with the music, without ever seeing to hurry.[6] She did this without any trick *rallentandi* on Lambert's part. In some of the few words Fonteyn ever wrote about Lambert, comparing his conducting to the musical laxity of the Russian ballet world, she said that he 'was not a man to be ordered about by a handful of ballet dancers. He understood ballet as a genuine marriage between music and dance, with music the senior partner.'[7]

Swan Lake was one of the ballets in which Fonteyn's musicality reached supreme heights, and it was in December 1937 that she danced both Odette and, for the first time, Odile. With Fonteyn, *Swan Lake* was a cumulative achievement. The moving reserve of Odette in Act Two was capped by the dangerous allure of Odile in Act Three, which, in turn, was capped by the emotional intensity of Odette in Act Four. The grand rhetoric of Tchaikovsky's score was expressed less in her face (as Odette, she developed a mask-like austerity around the cheeks and mouth) than in her line and phrasing. Some ballerinas make a glaring contrast between Odette and Odile, so that Siegfried is made to look silly in falling for Odile's flashy vampings, but with Fonteyn both roles were steeped in classical rigour – and Odile's behaviour to Siegfried was serious. Of her nineteenth-century roles, Odette–Odile was the one she changed the least, even though she danced it for over thirty-five years. By 1937, Fonteyn had the technique to attempt Odile's most celebrated bravura effect –

the thirty-two *fouetté* turns on pointe. In these, the ballerina turns repeatedly on one leg while the other propels her in a whiplash (*fouetté*) motion; ideally, the dancer should not travel an inch while turning. These turns had been virtually the only flawed area of Markova's technique, so that she soon learned to avoid ballets that required them. Fonteyn, whom they suited even less, went on doing them. They were part of the traditional choreography – and that was that. In this, as in so much, she epitomized British grit, and the Vic-Wells sense of personal subordination to a larger cause.

In January 1938, she danced in *Horoscope*. This new Lambert–Ashton ballet, expressing Lambert's fascination with astrology, showed the influence of the signs of the zodiac on two young lovers. Lambert dedicated the score to Fonteyn: the most public demonstration he ever made of his feeling for her. The ballet received more than twenty curtain calls on opening night, and was given sixteen performances during 1938 alone.

Throughout these years, Fonteyn continued to learn the awesome discipline of a ballerina's life. For her next major role she needed it. In February 1939, Sergueyev staged the full-length ballet

The Sleeping Princess (as *The Sleeping Beauty* was called in the 1920s and 1930s) for the Vic-Wells Ballet. This ballet, choreographed in St Petersburg in 1890 by Marius Petipa in close collaboration with the composer Tchaikovsky, had seldom been danced in the West; Princess Aurora gave Fonteyn the first evening-length role in which she had not seen Markova, indeed, had not seen any ballerina. It gave her less to act than any role she had tackled so far. Aurora celebrates her birthday; pricks her finger; swoons into a hundred-year sleep; appears as a beautiful but remote vision to Prince Charming; is woken by his kiss; dances a *grand pas de deux* with him at her own wedding. To a young ballerina who liked to absorb herself in the moment-by-moment stage reality of her roles, this was little to go on. The costumes and scenery were simple but unlovely. Fonteyn was approaching her twentieth birthday, and – as photographs show – at the chubbiest stage of her professional career.

She herself – somehow drawing from all her advisers and from her own musical intuition – established standards of musicality in *The Sleeping Princess* that are still pursued today. Fonteyn had a very strict sense of rhythm, and a potent sense of lyrical phrasing; she caught the breath of the music. Her first performance of it, revealing a new sparkle, brought her the greatest success of her career. As in the complete *Swan Lake*, her effect was cumulative. However fine her account of the Rose Adagio or the variation in the first act, she would then make a surpassingly elegant and poetic Vision in Act Two, only to shine with awakened maturity in the wedding of Act Three. And in every episode she lit up the ballet with her exquisite manners, both to her colleagues on stage and to her audience. Aurora became the signature role of her entire career.

FOUR

BALLET UNDER THE BOMBS
1939–45

Fonteyn had jumped splendidly through every hoop that de Valois and Ashton had held in front of her. They, in turn, rewarded her by making her the centrepiece of the repertory. *The Sleeping Princess*, for example, was given dozens of times between 1939 and 1942; Fonteyn was given every performance of Aurora save one, which went to Pamela May. All performances of Giselle were danced by Fonteyn until 1944, except some on tour by June Brae in 1941. Mary Honer danced a few performances of the full-length Odette–Odile in 1937–8, but during 1939 and 1940 the role was danced by Fonteyn alone. This established the pattern that was to be the making of Fonteyn, but was to be an insuperable problem for other ballerinas. Until the mid-1960s, Fonteyn was almost always first-cast, and she danced more performances of almost all her roles than anyone else. Has any other important ballet company in history rested so much for so many years upon the shoulders of one ballerina? In later years, several dancers felt undeniable frustration. Yet they admired Fonteyn's dancing and they admired her good manners, her professionalism, her discipline and her sense of humour.

In this period, however, the star of the company was Robert Helpmann, her partner in most ballets, and the most magnetic British dancer of the day. The Vic-Wells audience, which so often attended Vic-Wells plays and operas as well as ballets, adored the fact that Helpmann had started a supplementary career as an actor in the late 1930s. And, in the next few years, he was to consolidate yet further his hold over the ballet audience. Many people from that era testify to Helpmann's ability to monopolize all attention. No dancer complained; Helpmann was only too happy to encourage them to compete for the limelight.

When the outbreak of war was announced in 1939, the entire mood of life for Fonteyn and the

Vic-Wells Ballet changed overnight. Literally. That night, all the dancers were woken, in the strange bedrooms they had just occupied in or around Leeds, by an air-raid warning siren (a false alarm). The company was disbanded the next day; the rest of the tour was cancelled; the company's forthcoming season at Sadler's Wells was also called off. For a while it seemed that the company was to come to an end. However, a fortnight later, the company regrouped for a regional tour. Six evening performances and three matinees were given each week; Sundays were spent travelling by train to the next town. There was no orchestra; Constant Lambert and Hilda Gaunt accompanied performances on two pianos.

The company responded to war in ways both merry and serious. On this tour and on numerous tours that were to follow, the dancers larked about more than ever – in trains, on railway platforms, at their lodgings. Meanwhile, they were fervently rehearsing Ashton's third Liszt ballet, *Dante Sonata*. Ashton staged it as a plotless drama, a struggle between the Children of Light and the Children of Darkness. Fonteyn, Pamela May, Julia Farron and Michael Somes led those of Light, June Brae and

Helpmann those of Darkness. This was Ashton's first barefoot ballet. Fonteyn and Somes had 'one brief, heart-stopping moment of ecstasy when they ran towards a shaft of golden light, their bodies seeming to cry aloud, "The sun, the sun!"'[1] As the curtain fell, with the two opposed leading men held up high in a double crucifixion, Fonteyn was suddenly seen walking between the two groups and gesturing into infinity: a brief vision, as of Dante's Beatrice, bathed in light.

Also during the 'phony war' period, Ashton created *The Wise Virgins*, one of his first metaphysical ballets. To the music of Bach, the movingly serene choreography was, like that for *Dante Sonata*, without pointework and often without any use of academic ballet vocabulary. Fonteyn danced the Bride, in a mood of sustained quiet, rapture and wonder. Ashton here disclosed her gift for expressive stillness. Her soft and gentle solo spread a transportingly contemplative peace throughout the theatre.

In May 1940 the company visited Holland, in an exercise in wartime 'cultural propaganda'.[2] Audiences were enthusiastic, but, before the company's first week had ended, the Germans had invaded. Though the company reached England in safety, it had to leave behind scenery, costumes and music for the six ballets it had taken. *Horoscope* was, as a consequence, never seen again. For Lambert, the loss of so personal a ballet was hard to bear.

It was now that the most serious period of the war began. Male dancers began to disappear rapidly into the forces. Helpmann, as an Australian not required to sign up, remained the company's linchpin, but in several ballets Fonteyn often found herself being partnered by sixteen-year-old boys who were given roles far earlier than would usually have occurred. The company kept up its pattern of provincial tours, each lasting between eight and twelve weeks, alternating with London seasons of a similar length. Air-raid warnings became frequent and the British grew accustomed to them and to actual bombing. Sadler's Wells Theatre was soon commandeered as a rest centre for air-raid victims; the Old Vic and Sadler's Wells Theatres had to be administered from Lancashire. Although ballet shoes were still manufactured, the same few irreplaceable silk stockings had to be sent for repair again and again.

In 1941 the company gave its first season in its new London venue, the New Theatre (now the

Albery) in St Martin's Lane. At this theatre, as on tour, the Vic-Wells dancers gradually began to acquire a devoted new audience. Often air-raid signals would sound, but Fonteyn and Helpmann would carry on dancing . . . and, following their example, the audience would stay seated and enthralled. To many people during these war years, ballet became a prime source of spiritual sustenance.

Fonteyn, Helpmann, Lambert and de Valois held the company together with their commitment. In 1941 Pamela May suffered a serious knee injury. This, coupled with the birth of a son and the death of her young husband in war, kept her offstage for two years. June Brae, also newly wed, took leave to give birth to a daughter. Mary Honer, though still in her twenties, retired in 1942. This conferred a new isolation on Fonteyn. She began to develop a 'star complex' – soon abandoned when May, living in the grim reality of her recent loss, visited Fonteyn and told her plainly not to be pretentious.[3] Early in 1942 two striking new prospective ballerinas began to make their mark in performances: the lovely redhead Moira Shearer and the tall, spectacularly strong, fourteen-year-old Beryl Grey. In Ashton's absence, Helpmann began to choreograph, giving Fonteyn two impressive new roles in his masque *Comus* and his dramatic nightmare ballet *Hamlet*, both new in 1942. Fonteyn's stamina, already impressive, reached new peaks. It had to, for sometimes she had to dance two performances of *The Sleeping Princess* in a day. On some days she danced not only *Giselle* twice but also *Apparitions* once. Her partnership with Helpmann went from strength to strength. She was primarily a dancer who was never less than an effective actress; he was primarily an actor who was usually a stylish, seldom powerful, dancer. The contrast was what made their success.

Her relationship with Lambert continued. Various matters, however, put it under some strain. Lambert had always loved drink. Even before the war, his conducting had been occasionally the worse for its influence; now, as dancers and orchestra (if not audience) noticed, it became increasingly variable. Despite their deep rapport, Fonteyn knew she could not be Lambert's complete soulmate. She was not in his intellectual league, and the long hours she spent working and rehearsing meant that she could not always be at his side when he had the blues. For Lambert, there began to be, as his friend the pianist Angus Morrison has admitted, 'various affairs inside and outside the company'.[4] Ashton said, 'Margot loses her head but not her heart.' She remarked later, 'In truth I lost neither.'[5]

And yet high spirits often prevailed. Neither Lambert nor Fonteyn could tolerate pretension in others, which set the pattern for the company. Indeed, a sense of fun must have been among the things Lambert and Fonteyn most loved in each other. Once, in 1943, Fonteyn and Helpmann were invited to the Belle Vue Zoo in Manchester to name two zebras. Once there, however, Helpmann spotted a llama that bore, he insisted, so absolute a resemblance to himself that he had to confer his name on that instead. The two told Lambert of the fun they had had and that there was a solitary zebra without a name. Lambert phoned the zoo superintendant to request permission to come and name the zebra after himself. Permission was readily granted.

During the war, Mrs Hookham continued to be an exemplary ballet mother. On days when the Sadler's Wells dancers had no time to break between matinee and evening performances and remained in stage make-up, she helped to prepare food for everybody. The house that she and Fonteyn shared was blasted by a nearby bomb in 1944, while she was inside (Fonteyn was out). Fonteyn danced the next evening, albeit not in her best form, and the audience watched with enthusiasm even while 'robots' (pilotless German bombers) passed continuously overhead. As with the contralto Kathleen Ferrier, the war years made Fonteyn a British idol; like Ferrier, she expressed a beauty, a quality of heart, a state of grace and a devotion to her art that were, for all those who packed the theatres to see her, an oasis.

In 1943, Vera Volkova – whom Fonteyn had encountered in Shanghai – began to teach in London. Many dancers flocked to her classes, and found that she brought a revelatory logic to ballet exercises. Fonteyn was among them. Of all her teachers, Volkova proved the most important. She changed, among other things, the way Fonteyn used her feet, developing a proper use of their arches, and giving them a new strength. This exceptional humility and preparedness to re-build even the foundations of her art would mark Fonteyn well into her forties.

In 1945, the company toured Western Europe under the auspices of ENSA (the Entertainments

National Service Association). Paris filled Fonteyn, and all who had known it before 1940, with nostalgia. Here there was little food and less luxury, but the beauty of the city remained. Fonteyn was able to study again with her beloved Preobrajenska and the British visitors encountered a new generation of French dancers, one of whom was Roland Petit, then a nineteen-year-old, soon to make a big impact on the ballet world and on Fonteyn herself.

Later in 1945, Fonteyn fell ill and was unable to dance with the company on its winter tour of Germany. Dr Isaac Muende, the specialist treating her, became greatly concerned to prevent an infection on her face from leaving a serious scar. Using an entirely new technique, he injected the recently discovered drug penicillin straight into the point of infection – with complete success. When Fonteyn observed his anxiety about the scar, she said, 'Oh my feet are much more important than my face.' Muende, 'not believing I was so silly as to mean it,' treated her face with utmost delicacy, 'never realizing that, the stage being the only thing that mattered to me, I attached no importance to any blemish that would be invisible at a distance.'[6]

As always, Fonteyn's readiness to show herself up is both rare and endearing, as is her light touch in so doing. Other things, however, had been weighing on her mind. Lambert was ill – exhausted, spitting blood, emotionally unstable. He was not yet forty; Fonteyn was just twenty-six. She knew only too well that he had devoted years of his life to the Sadler's Wells Ballet, years in which he had composed too little music (and too little of that at his highest level), and she was deeply aware of her debt to his immersion in every aspect of the company's work. She knew this but she knew, as well, her own increasing incapacity to help him cope with the drastic emotional highs and lows of his life.

A TALE OF
TWO CITIES
1946–9

Frederick Ashton once came backstage to congratulate Fonteyn after a performance of a ballet of his that she had been dancing for years. 'Well, tonight was perfect,' he said, '*Why* was it perfect?' 'Because I remembered what you told me five years ago,' she replied. Ashton, telling this story, explained, 'She thought and thought about things, and unless they were really in her she couldn't do them. She had to really absorb.'[1] A key instance of this occurred in 1946.

The Sadler's Wells Ballet's sterling work through the war years now received its reward: it was made the resident ballet company of the Royal Opera House, Covent Garden. The ballet tradition of the great theatre (which had become a dance-hall during the war) was still associated with the great Russian ballet companies. Now an English company was to live there, and to open its régime, moreover, with a long series of performances of the Russian classic *The Sleeping Princess*. Or, rather, *The Sleeping Beauty*, as the ballet was rechristened at last. But could the three 'beauties' (Fonteyn, Pamela May and Moira Shearer), or indeed anyone one else in the company, project successfully into the new/old theatre? Helpmann, performing both as Carabosse (in the Prologue and Act One) and as the Prince (in Acts Two and Three), took naturally to his new surroundings — but it was chiefly his stage presence and his power of mime gesture that succeeded. Fonteyn had to make her dancing reach into the opera house; Aurora has few moments of mime. When she led the opening performance in February 1946, she showed that she had greatly matured in grace, footwork and freshness since 1939. It was nonetheless apparent, as Mary Clarke wrote, 'that she had yet to take the measure of the great auditorium and project her performance to its outermost areas'.[2]

Decades later, Ashton talked about what followed.

I went all over the house . . . and I said 'You're *still* not registering. I don't know what's the matter. I've been upstairs, I've been downstairs,' and then one day she held a pose a fraction longer and I went back and I said 'I've got it. You've been used to a small theatre. You've got to *hold* everything much more, so as to register. . . . You mustn't go rushing too quickly. Show everything clearly.'[3]

But it was up to Fonteyn to do this without any change in musical tempi.

Nothing did she master better than her first entrance. The new production of *The Sleeping Beauty* had beautifully picturesque designs by Oliver Messel. For Act One he arranged an astonishing first appearance for Aurora. All the characters onstage turned back to look at her. Entering, she ran right along a path at the back; struck an arabesque; ran right off again, on the opposite side; and at once dashed back on, at top speed, to the main stage, where she began to dance. At once she filled her audience 'with the fresh youthfulness of the young Princess, the radiant gaiety of all the fairy tale heroines of all the world's literature compressed into one'.[4]

Ashton particularly coached Fonteyn in the grand adagio of Act Three. She refined yet further her account of the central passage in which she suddenly folds herself on the floor at her prince's feet; sitting up and taking his hand, she places one pointe decisively on the floor before her and steps onto it; then – very slowly and still supported by his hand – she draws herself up on that pointe, her leg slowly straightening as she rises. Her other leg is angled behind her and finally, as she arrives, her whole body glows in another of Aurora's radiant signature *attitudes*. Then, to bring the musical phrase to its climax, she lets go of the prince's hand and, still on pointe, explodes into a triumphant, sustained arabesque. With Fonteyn, this grand *crescendo* – which bears resemblance to little else in classical ballet – summed up much about the whole ballet: the idea of her sleep, his arrival and her awakening; and the chivalry whereby he assisted her to grow to glory.

Ashton's work on *The Sleeping Beauty* with Fonteyn was part of a new phase in his career, when he immersed himself in pure dance classicism. He now took the first three Sadler's Wells Ballet Auroras – Fonteyn, May, Shearer – and three men – Michael Somes, Brian Shaw, Henry Danton – and began to work on a ballet that expressed the metaphysical thoughts that had fascinated him during the war. The result, *Symphonic Variations*, to César Franck's score, is a ballet that impressed almost all who saw it as Ashton's greatest work to date; and Fonteyn's role in it was, for many British observers, her finest of all. In its harmonies of line and musicality, this ballet expressed a great deal without ever making any specific communication. The chaste and sculptural movement of the women is thawed by the advent of the men. Dancers move in various combinations and solos, now matching, now anticipating the music; the fleet, bright solo for Fonteyn is one of the passages when Ashton most intensely responds to the voice of the solo piano.

Sometimes dancers at the centre – Fonteyn and Somes, for example, holding a position of limpid classical line – are motionless, while others dance around them; sometimes dancers stand still on the perimeters of the dancing space while others dance within it. At one point, while all other five dancers move, Fonteyn alone held her still pose, standing in the corner of the stage – like, said a friend, 'the still centre of the world'. This stationary pose was also the ballet's strongest statement of meditation amid action. Observers were held by the calm and rapt gaze of her eyes, up and out into the auditorium, but were affected, above all, by the glorious repose of the area at the base of her neck. This repose, which gave utter serenity to the way she held her head and shoulders, was worthy of Praxiteles, and was one of the hallmarks of her classicism.

Ballet after ballet, old or new, was brought into the Covent Garden repertory during the course of 1946 and 1947; Fonteyn was kept busy. Early in 1947 she fell ill with 'flu; on her recovery, she still felt 'stale and uninspired'.[5] Going to de Valois, she asked permission for a few weeks' leave of absence, to study in Paris. By this time, her relationship with Constant Lambert had broken down irretrievably. His drinking had grown markedly worse and he had begun a new relationship. In Paris, Fonteyn found precisely what she needed. A Russian teacher, Boris Kniaseff, gave her renewed confidence in her dancing; she also studied with Preobrajenska and Kschessinskaya; she began to converse in French with the dancers of Les Ballets des Champs-Elysées, whom she had met in Paris in 1945 and again in their 1946 London season; and she started an affair with the French dancer-choreographer Roland Petit.

Petit was five years younger than Fonteyn, had the same black eyes as she (and Tito de Arias) did and was already setting tongues clucking with such innovative ballets as *Le Jeune Homme et la mort*. 'We developed a deep but harmless crush on each other, born of the mutual stimulation of his inventive imagination and my restrained classicism,' she wrote later. 'He told me I should leave the Sadler's Wells Ballet, where I was too restricted, and get out and dance new, exciting ballets. I told him he needed the stability of the Paris Opéra from which he had broken away. Neither of us took the other's advice.'[6] He, speaking later of the ebullience he had helped to release in her, said simply, 'I opened the door'.[7] He took her for the first time to Christian Dior, where she found an evening dress in which 'I had never felt so elegant in my life'.[8] Fonteyn had always been immaculately well-dressed; from now on, she became an international icon of fashion.

Her energy renewed, Fonteyn returned to work with the Sadler's Wells Ballet. The company's long tour (August–October 1947) included the first Edinburgh Festival, Belgium, Czechoslovakia, Poland and Norway. In the following weeks and months, the Iron Curtain descended to bar Poland and Czechoslovakia from the West for the next forty-two years. During the tour, another iron curtain had already descended in Fonteyn's life. Surprise news reached the dancers that Lambert had married Isabel Delmer. Fonteyn, according to

Ashton, 'just cut out the whole episode. Sewed herself up and became virginal again.'[9]

She was soon, however, to forge a good professional relationship with Lambert and, sooner or later, they were behaving like old friends, albeit while preserving a greater distance. In January 1948, Lambert conducted the first performances of Ashton's new masterwork, *Scènes de ballet*, an elaborate and plotless study in high-density classicism, to Stravinsky's recent score. This work, full of complex geometries, rhythms, and overlaid with a veneer of chic, was strange for Fonteyn. She found it hard to grasp a core of meaning behind its high-style atmosphere, although its choreography still shows today how Ashton intended to display her current level of brilliance and her new Parisienne elegance.

Fonteyn was starting two new phases of her life: life after Lambert, and life after Helpmann. Helpmann, although he still partnered her at times, was working more and more in the spoken theatre and she was adjusting to performing the nineteenth-century ballets with Somes, who hitherto had partnered her almost solely in Ashton ballets (as he did in *Scènes de ballet*). Somes had virile beauty, as Helpmann never had, and he had the same handsome carriage as Fonteyn's. He had little of Helpmann's wit or flair, however, and took a very long time to develop as a partner. As for life after Lambert: Fonteyn took leave in spring 1948 to appear in Paris as a guest artist with Roland Petit's new company, Les Ballets de Paris. The Fonteyn–Petit relationship was sexual, but also creative: she loved the new ballet, *Les Demoiselles de la nuit*, that he made for her. She also danced excerpts from *The Sleeping Beauty* in magnificent costumes by Pierre Balmain. Back in London, Fonteyn's dancing was seen to have acquired new lustre. The American critic Edwin Denby discussed her change of style as a 'revolution' that she now began to lead against the Anglo-Saxon 'thinness and meagreness of temperament' around her.[10]

In November 1948, however, at the first performance of Ashton's latest ballet, *Don Juan*, she tore a ligament in her ankle. The next day, her foot was in a plaster cast. To console herself, she soon escaped to Paris. France, however, could not cure her depression; she discusses this injury in her *Autobiography* as 'a major personal crisis'.[11] Why so?

There were now three younger ballerinas – Beryl Grey, Moira Shearer, Violetta Elvin – who were more than ready to step into her shoes. All three were attractive; all had strong technical accomplishment. Grey's warmth and technical ease made her a darling of the gallery; the glamorous Elvin had replaced Fonteyn, successfully, in *Don Juan*; and the film of *The Red Shoes*, released that year, was making Moira Shearer a bigger name than Fonteyn. Behind them were Nadia Nerina and Svetlana Beriosova, perhaps more gifted yet.

Shearer tells the story that, before making her debut as Giselle in 1948, she studied the role with Tamara Karsavina (who had danced the ballet with Nijinsky for Diaghilev in 1910), and that de Valois had been incensed at the changes Shearer had interpolated into the choreographic text, until Shearer told her their source. Whereupon de Valois brought in Karsavina to coach Fonteyn – but no other ballerina – in *Giselle*.[12] Shearer reserves all her criticism for de Valois here; still, one must wonder just how free Fonteyn can have been from complicity in this arrangement.

At the time of Fonteyn's injury, Ashton had just started to rehearse *Cinderella*, his (and Britain's) first three-act ballet. When first he planned a continuous run of *Cinderella* performances, Fonteyn told him that she could not dance a three-act ballet every night. He therefore announced that Fonteyn and Shearer would

The first photograph to be published of the future Margot Fonteyn (right) in 1931, when she was almost twelve. She danced in 'Dragon Sprites' with Veronica Clifton at a concert given in April by the Royal Society of St George, Shanghai. (*Dancing Times*)

Fonteyn with Frederick Ashton: theirs was the longest ballerina-choreographer collaboration in history. Here they dance as Debutante and Dago in the Tango of his *Façade* (1931), in its new 1940 production. She danced this role until her sixtieth birthday in 1979. (V&A Picture Library)

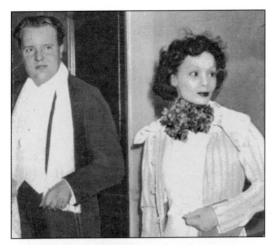

Constant Lambert with his first wife Florence. They are arriving at Covent Garden for the British first night of Weinberger's opera, *Schwanda the Bagpiper*, in 1934. In 1937, when Florence discovered the seriousness of the affair between Fonteyn and Lambert, she left him. (Mander & Mitchenson Theatre Collection)

Fonteyn as Woman in Ball Dress and Robert Helpmann as the Poet in *Apparitions* (1936). Lambert arranged this ballet's three-scene scenario and Liszt score with this leading couple in mind. As choreographed by Ashton, designed by Cecil Beaton and conducted by Lambert, it proved one of the biggest successes to date for the Vic-Wells Ballet. Fonteyn was sixteen. She last danced *Apparitions* in 1953, in memorial to Lambert.
(Gordon Anthony/V&A Picture Library)

Fonteyn, partnered by Michael Somes, in *Swan Lake*. Somes was her chief partner throughout the 1950s. This action photograph shows the particular tragic intensity of her line as the Swan Queen, Odette. (Michael Wood)

This photograph of Fonteyn in *The Sleeping Beauty* shows the ideal loveliness of her body in ballet: notably the radiant proportions of her limbs and also her slender waist, the fullness of her fingertips and her 'wonderfully alert head'. (Gordon Anthony/V&A Picture Library)

Symphonic Variations (1946). Here Ashton showed Fonteyn's line in new ways, fascinatingly complemented by the lines of Sophie Fedorovich's designs. A pure dance work, it mixed stillness and movement, music and geometry to sublime metaphysical effect. Here Fonteyn is lifted by Michael Somes; Moira Shearer and Henry Danton are also seen. (Baron/Camera Press)

Tito (Roberto) de Arias and Fonteyn at their wedding in Paris in 1955. Despite political scandals and a period of difficulty in the 1960s, Fonteyn took her marriage vows seriously. She renewed her devotion when Tito was crippled in an assassination attempt in 1964. The couple are buried beside each other. (Hulton-Getty Picture Library)

In *Ondine* (1958), Ashton made a three-act ballet for Fonteyn as a water-nymph. Here she is seen for the first time on dry land, dancing in surprise and delight at having a shadow. For many, this solo was the quintessence of the playful spontaneity and sweetness of manner that was most loved in Fonteyn. (Houston Rogers/V&A Picture Library)

Daphnis and Chloë (1951) was a ballet Fonteyn had long hoped Ashton would choreograph for her. Her Chloë was a child of nature, surrounded by a loving community of friends, at one with her landscape. Here her lover Daphnis (David Blair in this 1961 photograph) lifts her, while their friends surround them, shortly after she has joyfully returned from her abduction by pirates.

(Houston Rogers/V&A Picture Library)

La Bayadère, with Rudolf Nureyev. In this scene, which Nureyev taught to the Royal Ballet production, Solor (Nureyev) dreams an opium-induced vision of a realm of Shades, a *ballet blanc*. Here his beloved Nikiya (Fonteyn), although now dead, returns to him, transformed from her mortal existence as an Indian temple dancer (*bayadère*) into an example of transcendent ballet classicism. The sculptural elegance of Fonteyn's line is shown to perfection. (Leslie E. Spatt)

In Panama, with one of her dogs, in 1990, the year before her death. Fonteyn discovered her love for the sea in early childhood; it gave her 'the sense of total freedom and happiness' and effectively restored her faith in lasting values. At the time of this photograph, Fonteyn was a widow and had been undergoing treatment for cancer. (Vivienne Ventura)

alternate in the title role. The whole situation had made Fonteyn, as she herself admits, 'ill at ease and defensive'. She goes so far as to say that 'Perhaps it was not wholly accidental, therefore, when I slipped and fell during that performance of *Don Juan*'.[13] Now, with Fonteyn's injury, Ashton also put Shearer on in the 'Fonteyn' performances of *Cinderella* too. It was probably at this time that, following the advice of Petit (who had had a nose job himself), Fonteyn decided to have her nose resculpted. She also let friends from Maison Dior continue to supervise her clothes and she experimented with several new coiffures. All this notwithstanding, she now recognized, sadly, that she had no direction in her life save ballet.

How did she solve the problem of her career? She went back, as soon as possible, to dancing. She at once tackled Cinderella and made it her own. Though Ashton always expressed his admiration for Shearer's performance, and though he coached other dancers in this ballet until the last year of his life, Cinderella became one of the roles in which he found himself unable to help superimposing Fonteyn's image on top of all her successors.

SIX

THE APOGEE
1949–53

Fonteyn reached her thirtieth birthday in 1949. By now she had danced in several European countries, always with success, and she had been hailed by audiences who had also seen the other leading Western ballerinas of the day. In summer 1949, she appeared in two more countries, Italy (Florence) and Denmark (Copenhagen). Now an announcement was made that the Sadler's Wells Ballet would appear at New York's Metropolitan Opera House in October, and would then tour America and Canada. For three months prior to this appearance, Fonteyn went into an unearthly calm, which was, she later admitted, her way of coping with the hysteria of the company's preparations for New York, and with the most appalling stage fright of her life.

Or, rather, calm was her way of preparing herself to take the town by storm. Calm, and hard work.

During a month of appearances by the company that summer, she made time to practise the Rose Adagio for two hours each day. When she balanced on pointe in the famous series of *attitudes*, her arms raised *en couronne*, she insisted that each prince should stand at a distance from her, only gradually approaching her. Steadily she worked to make it seem that, when finally she brought down her hand and placed it in the next prince's clasp, it was because she chose to, not because she needed to.

Opening night, 9 October, was Indian summer weather in New York, the hottest day of the year. Every one of the Met's 3,459 seats was taken; the boxes and standing room were packed; there was a vast queue for returns; the pressure of traffic caused complete gridlock near the theatre. Lambert's conducting, Messel's designs, Beryl Grey's Lilac Fairy, Ashton's Carabosse: these all helped to make the evening a triumph. And then, ten minutes into Act One, Fonteyn entered. Thanks largely to Tchaikovsky, Messel and Lambert, the audience began to clap long before she appeared. By the time she was on stage, the sound hit her like deafening thunder. But the audience was no longer applauding just the music and the production. It was now applauding her. As the critic Doris Hering recollects:

> The first impression is . . . of the wide-set dark eyes; and that wonderfully alert head . . . and the gentle shoulders; and the arabesque that had no end. It was not finite, it floated. And then, when she got to the spindle dance, and she circled the stage in that kind of windswept way – well, I was totally under her spell.[1]

Harold Turner, who had been partnering Fonteyn since 1935, said that he had never known her 'so relaxed, so completely without strain in the Rose Adagio', in which he was the first of the four princes to partner her; the ballerina Maria Tallchief, although she possessed an allegro technique far more brilliant than Fonteyn's, was elated by the entire evening, and by Fonteyn above all; and Mary Clarke, who had watched Fonteyn's London performances for ten years, wrote that it was the performance of her career to date.[2] Fonteyn began to be hailed as a ballerina among ballerinas. She had further triumphs during the season and was to keep on astounding New Yorkers, as Aurora and in other ballets, on visits with the same ballet company over the next twenty-three years.

Two experiences during this New York season constituted a turning point in Fonteyn's perception of herself. Helpmann and she were invited to visit the actress Katharine Hepburn, who had enjoyed international celebrity since the early 1930s. Hepburn, opening the door of her house, said to Fonteyn, 'Oh! I am so excited to meet you!' Fonteyn was taken aback. The great movie star excited to meet this foreign dancer? Then *Time* magazine put her on its cover. 'Perhaps these two occurrences helped to bring about my identification with the Margot Fonteyn who is always something of a mystery to me,' wrote Fonteyn in her autobiography. 'At least I decided to enjoy the benefits of my ambiguous relationship to her.'[3]

The next spring, at Covent Garden, Fonteyn was given the leading role in George Balanchine's *Ballet Imperial*. Balanchine's way of working was a revelation to the British dancers. He could play the entire score on the piano and he knew exactly what he wanted from them. But his ballet's style proved yet more alien to Fonteyn than any choreography she had attempted to date, and technically far more exacting. Balanchine found Moira Shearer — who was to lead the ballet's second cast — more prepared than Fonteyn to take on the crucial off-balance features of his style. Fonteyn, who danced the premiere on 5 April 1950, stubbornly insisted on dancing always securely on her balance, thus missing a key feature of Balanchine classical style. The velocity and elevation that this ballet demanded were also beyond her capacity, as was the fact that the ballet had none of the sublimated sense of characterization that marked the plotless ballets of her beloved Ashton. *Ballet Imperial* was the first classical ballet to elude her completely.

Fonteyn's position was now such that this blip in her career was soon forgotten. 'These were my prime years.'[4] With the ballet-master Harijs Plučis and with her partner Michael Somes, Fonteyn completely re-examined her roles during the 1950s. Her excellence in bravura passages varied – some Rose Adagios in *Beauty* were tense, the thirty-two *fouetté* turns in *Lac* travelled forwards a good deal at some performances – but were chiefly to her own high standards. Most important, as Moira Shearer has been the first to stress, is that Fonteyn's general level of excellence never once sank beneath a very high level.[5] Whether in the 1940s, 1950s, or 1960s, even Fonteyn's least successful performances were, almost without exception, always marked by consistently firm technique and by devout artistry. She immersed herself in her role, in her music and in her responsibility to the audience.

In 1951, Ashton began rehearsals for a ballet that Fonteyn had long hoped for – *Daphnis and Chloë*, to the Ravel score. Rather than re-imagine ancient Greece, he decided to present the story in simple contemporary dress. Gods and mortals inhabit the same landscape, which Ashton achieved without nostalgia for a bygone period. As Chloë, Fonteyn was so at one with her community and the landscape that she made a tragic effect in the scene when pirates held her captive. Dancing a solo with her wrists bound, 'Chloë confronts her captors with the unspeakableness of their crime against her. From Fonteyn,' Arlene Croce wrote later, 'I had the impression that the crime was as much or more against nature, and that she couldn't understand how it could be happening.'[6] Reconciled in the final scene with Daphnis and their companions, this Chloë became the lyrical embodiment of bliss. Chloë was one of the two roles that made Fonteyn happiest; the second – Ondine – was some years in the future.

Ashton's relationship with Fonteyn was now that of Pygmalion and Galatea. She was the work of art, he the artist. While he was proud of having 'made' her, she also astounded him by the beauty she revealed. By now she was far more famous than he. Later, he would sometimes demonstrate possessiveness, claiming how much he had contributed to her career, talking of having coached her accounts of the classical ballets and, indeed, her curtain calls. Yet she was happy to give him full credit. In 1986, she wrote from Panama to tell him, 'There is really NO ONE like you. How incredibly lucky I was in my career to fall into your magic hands. Imagine where I would have been otherwise with my no elevation, no extension, no instep and feeble pirouettes!'[7] Meanwhile he would describe her with wonder: 'She has the body of Venus and the mind of Minerva.'[8]

Since 1930, Constant Lambert had talked of a *Tiresias* ballet; now he composed it. Tiresias is the person who, having lived both as a man and as a woman, can answer the question: which sex most enjoys sex? Answer: the female. Lambert planned the female Tiresias as Fonteyn's role: a fact that speaks for itself about their former sexual relationship. When the ballet had its premiere in July 1951, her scene, by all accounts, contained the most intimately felt parts of his composition and of Ashton's choreography. Otherwise, the ballet was too long and was obviously flawed. Lambert was by now a sick man.

Six weeks later, he was dead. Fonteyn, Ashton and the ballet company were up at the Edinburgh Festival, where they danced *Tiresias* with a fervour worthy to commemorate him. Then, and in the ballet's subsequent performances, Fonteyn, wrote Mary Clarke, 'danced as one possessed; she had a passionate intensity in this ballet which she has not equalled in any other role'.[9] (Typically, in her autobiography, Fonteyn skips right past *Tiresias*, Lambert's death and the rest of the year.) The next year, *Apparitions* was revived at Covent Garden – surely so that Fonteyn and the company could dance a further memorial to Lambert. (In its final scene, after the despair and death of the artist hero, his muse arrives, to mourn him with greater tenderness than she had revealed during his fevered life.) In the meantime, however, Fonteyn rested her severely injured left foot as soon as the Edinburgh engagement ended; the injury kept her offstage for five months. At a memorial service for Lambert, she was seen to be deeply in grief.

It is remarkable how often Fonteyn's stage persona was, as Arlene Croce put it, 'indomitably chaste'.[10] This was what made her Odette so moving; the drama seemed, in part, to be about her virginity. In Ashton's next ballet for her – the three-act *Sylvia*, new in September 1952 – Fonteyn reverted to chastity. Sylvia is Amazonian, the leader of the huntresses who follow the moon-goddess, Diana. She rejects love, but then gets her comeuppance when she is penetrated by the arrow of the love god, Eros. She loses her heart to the man she has rejected, Aminta, and, after various plot developments, she is finally united with him. The ballet, set to the glorious 1876 score by Léo Delibes, celebrated Fonteyn's virtuosity, probably now at its zenith. In the dance to the famous *pizzicato* solo, Ashton showed off her feet as never before, making her hop on pointe (a favourite device in his choreography for women) as he had hitherto refrained from doing. The ballet, though it had incidental flaws, was a popular success for ten years.

Two months after the premiere, Fonteyn was on tour when a sore throat and fever stopped her from dancing. A shrewd young doctor diagnosed diphtheria, which, in due course, paralysed parts of her body for weeks. Again, she was absent for five months. This time, the seriousness of her illness – of which she makes light in her memoirs – caused immense concern among the ballet audience.

When finally she returned to the stage, her performance received one of the great ovations in the history of Covent Garden. Not that she had danced so remarkably that night; but she was back where she belonged. Much of Fonteyn's greatness lay in her relationship with her ballet company, and in her constant sense of personal subordination to a cause greater than herself. It was this 'objectivity', as Edwin Denby put it, that so often caused observers to shed or feel tears at her performances – that, and not sentimentality in her interpretation.[11] After this performance, more than fifty bouquets were laid at her feet; many of her colleagues cheered from the auditorium; house staff shouted 'Margot!'; and the general public's applause was a vast tide of affection. David Webster, general administrator of the Royal Opera House, was among the many who wept. When asked, 'What on earth is the matter?', he replied, 'If you don't understand, you certainly don't deserve to be told.'[12]

SEVEN

'A MULTIPLICITY OF INTERESTS'
1953–61

In September 1953 – during her second New York performance on the five-month Sadler's Wells Ballet tour of America – Tito de Arias re-entered Fonteyn's life. It had been fourteen years since they had met. He was now the delegate for his native Panama to the United Nations; and he had become fat, married, and the father of three children. Yet, within twenty-four hours of meeting her again, he proposed marriage to Fonteyn.[1] He bombarded her with flowers, with champagne, with chauffeur-driven limousine treatment, with lavish restaurant meals and parties that included the friends of hers he knew from Cambridge days, with jewels, with a fur coat; and meanwhile he lost weight rapidly.

Above all, Arias knew how to hunt Fonteyn, and how to keep hunting her. He maintained the pressure on her, right through the American tour, even reaching her by telegram when she thought herself safe from him on a three-day train journey. 'I felt hunted and desperate,' she writes. Imagery of the hunt that finds love is part of *Swan Lake*, *The Sleeping Beauty* and *Sylvia*; Fonteyn must have felt the parallels between life and art. As Odette, in particular, only gradually did she allow her frozen heart to thaw. Fonteyn had remained, deep down, inviolable. She had allied herself to her ballet company and to her mother; for no man – and there had been other affairs since those with Lambert and Petit – had she ever made a single serious compromise to her career.

How much did Fonteyn ever surrender herself to the conventional idea of marriage? She made it clear that she wanted no children, that she intended to continue a champagne lifestyle, that her career would continue. Did she know much of his political ambitions? She may well have seen a future for herself as a President's wife; Arias aspired to no less. The Eva Perón of Panama: that would be a part worth playing!

Her wedding did not take place until February 1955. The contradictions within her are perhaps summed up by the two roles she had danced on the previous day, Saturday 5 February. At the evening performance, she danced Chloë in *Daphnis* – her most loving role to date. When she made her final entrance, seated on the shoulder of Michael Somes – in what is anyway among the most exuberant and life-affirming of ballet finales – a shower of rose petals fell onto the stage (a very Ashton touch), and the dancers released streamers and confetti. That afternoon, however, she had danced a drastically different role: the Firebird. (It was also this role she danced immediately upon return from honeymoon.)

Fonteyn had been coached as the Firebird in 1954 by Tamara Karsavina, who had created the role for the choreographer Mikhail Fokine in 1910. She found Karsavina's words revealing: 'Forget your graces. The Firebird is powerful, hard to manage, rebellious.'[2] In 1978, when coaching the ballerina Monica Mason in the role, Fonteyn used further memories of Karsavina's words:

Apparently, according to the Russian folklore, Firebirds actually ate men. She absolutely was a man-eater. So the Prince doesn't really know what he has caught, but the Firebird knows. And she said that Karsavina had said from the moment the Prince catches her, she hates him. . . . You hate him, and you even hate the fact that you have to ask him to release you. You have to plead, but you plead without losing any of your dignity or your feeling of self-preservation.[3]

The twelve months leading up to Fonteyn's marriage were exceptionally busy, bringing, 'for the first time, a multiplicity of interests into my life'. She danced ('which is a full-time occupation') and she set up a new home ('which is another full-time occupation').[4] Arias was appointed the next Panamanian Ambassador to the Court of St James and was to take up the post after their wedding. She learned and danced *The Firebird*; and she succeeded, at Ninette de Valois's behest, the seventy-five-year-old Adeline Genée as President of the Royal Academy of Dancing. Though she took the RAD on in the belief that she was to be a mere figurehead, she soon became absorbed into the complex proceedings of this institution, which sets standards and examinations for dancers and teachers around the world.

After her wedding and honeymoon, Fonteyn started on her prestigious new responsibilities as an ambassador's wife ('it was another role for her',[5] her friend Pamela May has said), while keeping up her familiar responsibilities as a ballerina. Her dancing's high summer continued. Somes set her off to perfection: as the dancer Annette Page later said, 'He was completely there for her and sort of melted behind her so that you were not aware of her being supported'.[6] In 1956, the company became the Royal Ballet, as it has since remained, and its prima ballerina, aged thirty-six, was made Dame Margot Fonteyn (Dame Commander, Order of the British Empire). Ashton, who had made several short vehicles for Fonteyn in recent years, now created *Birthday Offering* to show off the company's seven leading female dancers, all crowned and bejewelled, and their male partners. Fonteyn danced the last of the seven female variations, into which, as a private joke to mark her new job at the RAD, Ashton put in an unusual step, the *pas de bourrée à cinq pas*, peculiar to the RAD syllabus. He also gave her and Somes a magical *pas de deux*.

Since 1949, she had been widely hailed as the greatest dancer in the world – with one exception.

Reports of the Bolshoi ballerina Galina Ulanova been leaking out from Russia since the war. When Ulanova made her Western debut at the Maggio Musicale in Florence in 1951, Vera Volkova, Violetta Elvin and Fonteyn's mother travelled to see her, along with several eminent critics, one of whom, Beryl de Zoete, wrote, 'From the first moment of her appearance something happened which upset all previous standards of perfection'.[7] In September 1956, Ulanova and the Bolshoi came to Covent Garden – it was the company's first tour to the West. Fonteyn was overwhelmed, and at once began to absorb the *cantilena* and the Stanislavskian lessons of Ulanova's dance-acting. At her very next performance, in *Sylvia*, the critic Clive Barnes detected a new, Ulanova-like identification with her role.[8]

That year, Ashton had begun preparing a new three-act ballet for her, *Ondine*. This, a work conceived in the neo-Romanticism of the day and probably intensely coloured by the Bolshoi's *Romeo*, was the only full evening ballet he ever made to a commissioned score; the composer was Hans Werner Henze. *Ondine* saw Fonteyn in her element: a water-nymph, 'naïve, shy, loyal and loving', spontaneous and capricious, fascinated by the unknown, first seen emerging from a fountain, so at ease in the sea that she laughs at a storm, and reluctantly rising to tragic heights as she gives her lover the fatal kiss he craves.[9] She said to Ashton, 'Things you've been trying to get me to do all my life, I'm at last beginning to understand.'[10] He revealed her phrasing at its most liquid, and – particularly in the solo she does on entry, dancing first in delight at being on dry land for the first time and then in astonished discovery of having a shadow – he made his greatest statement of her ability to make an entrancing world out of her solitude on stage. As in all her three-act roles, she underwent a change during the ballet. 'The fey creature of the first two acts is replaced by a woman who has known cruelty and suffering.'[11]

Increasingly, apart from her tours with the Royal Ballet, Fonteyn toured abroad, either as guest artist with foreign companies or with a small group of other Royal dancers. Between 1955 and 1958, she danced in Finland, Sweden, Monte Carlo, Norway, South Africa (performing on a raft on a lake in the Johannesburg Zoo before an audience of 6,000), Australia and Germany. (The delight of travel is a theme that occupies much space in her autobiography and inspires her to her finest writing.) In April 1959, after a long tour of Japan and New Zealand in which communication had been difficult, she went to Panama to spend two weeks' holiday with Arias.

'From the second year of our marriage,' she writes, 'he was more and more absorbed in his idea for a revolution, his sixth, in Panama.'[12] (His *sixth*. How mildly she notes that number.) However, she writes that she had little idea that he was now about to put his plans into action. Next, the plans failed. Fonteyn – after a week sailing with Arias in a gunboat – found herself placed under arrest, put into jail and then deported. (Meanwhile she had sent Arias off to escape, which he managed successfully.)

News broke while she was flying to New York, where she was met by dozens of pressmen, waiting for her on the tarmac. She rose to the occasion with courteous, steely, good-humoured cool. In response to a pointed question, she said (a sudden inspiration): 'You can read the answer to that in the papers.'[13] Laughter all round: whereupon Fonteyn had the press on her side. Fonteyn's long chapter in her autobiography about the attempted *coup* and its consequences has the reader on her side too; it has tenderness, humour, excitement, pathos. Yet it is an oddly irresponsible account, determinedly denying accountability. Denial, indeed, was integral to the Fonteyn persona. With this Panama episode, as with her affair with Lambert and as with later episodes in her life, she decided on her severely edited version of events, and clung to it faithfully.

While the brouhaha was calming down, she had her fortieth birthday. She did not suppose she would dance more than another year, she writes, and yet, as she acknowledges, she was dancing more than ever before. When a friend asked why she was working so hard, Fonteyn replied lightly, 'Guns don't come cheap'.[14] She had already learned that Arias had little money and that she had to pay for the champagne lifestyle with which he had lured her into marriage. Now she had to pay for his political escapades too. It was at this time that the Royal Ballet put up the price of tickets for Fonteyn performances. When she protested to the management that this practice put her in the same situation as certain visiting guest artists who came only for limited seasons, she found that soon afterwards, in July 1959, she was officially made a guest artist. Nonetheless, the Royal Ballet and Covent Garden remained her base, and she was to give them the majority of her performances for years to come.

Fonteyn always revered the Russian tradition of ballet. In 1961, she and the Royal Ballet were invited to dance in both St Petersburg and Moscow. This was something about which she had long fantasized. She and her colleagues enjoyed huge success in the opening-night *Ondine*. But not in *The Sleeping Beauty*. 'I think I gave my worst ever performance the night I danced it at the Kirov. It was not the general public's judgement I feared, but that of the Russian dancers and teachers.'[15] It was a difficult time in Fonteyn's career. The left foot she had injured in 1951 had given her increasing trouble. Since it was on that foot she had to execute the thirty-two *fouetté* turns of *Swan Lake*, she had stopped dancing that ballet in 1959. Just before the Russian tour, her doctor tried a manipulation of her foot under anaesthesia. The results were excellent and, as the Russian tour progressed, she found herself regaining both confidence and skill.

For the opening night in Moscow, the audience included Ulanova and two of the Bolshoi's other leading ballerinas, Maya Plisetskaya and Olga Lepeshinskaya. Fonteyn's Ondine made the Russians realize, wrote Natalia Roslavleva, 'from the very first encounter that she belongs to the numbered ranks of the greatest ballerinas of our time'.[16] *The Sleeping Beauty* enjoyed great success there with each of its three ballerinas, the Muscovites throwing flowers that, 'in the case of Margot Fonteyn, formed a complete carpet on the proscenium'.[17] Even so, despite great admiration for *Ondine* and for all her dancing, Fonteyn did not receive the kind of accolades that came her way elsewhere. The memory of her dancing there was long held in love, but Russia was the one country that she did not quite conquer.

EIGHT

'JUST YOU TRY'
1961–5

While the Royal Ballet was in Russia, the Kirov Ballet was touring Paris and London. In the Paris airport, the dancer Rudolf Nureyev defected. Aged twenty-three, he did not immediately find a career in the West, especially as the Russian authorities tried to exert diplomatic pressure on those companies which employed him. Fonteyn's friend Colette Clark, however, now had the idea of inviting him to appear at the November 1961 gala for the Royal Academy of Dancing. Clark tracked Nureyev down in Copenhagen, where he was studying with Fonteyn's old teacher and friend, Vera Volkova. Nureyev, with the double arrogance of both youth and a Russian star, told Volkova that he wanted to dance with Fonteyn. Volkova passed on her opinion that Nureyev was a genius. Fonteyn cabled back to Volkova: 'Delighted to have Nureyev come to London but I can't dance with him. I already have a partner.'[1] Nureyev, though initially crushed, quickly negotiated (and obtained) the American ballerina Rosella Hightower as his partner, *and* a solo to be created for him by none other than Frederick Ashton.

When Nureyev arrived in London, Fonteyn and Clarke watched him rehearse in the theatre. Although his intense seriousness and his superhigh energy had them in stitches of laughter, they took to him wholeheartedly. Soon Ninette de Valois decided that Nureyev should dance Albrecht in *Giselle* with the Royal Ballet. Would Fonteyn like to dance the ballet with him? Her initial reaction was that it would be 'like mutton dancing with lamb'. However, when she discussed it that evening with Arias (as she is careful to inform readers of her *Autobiography*), they concluded that Nureyev was bound to be the sensation of 1962 and that Fonteyn 'had better get on the bandwagon or else get out'.[2]

To 'get out' was a serious option. She had always thought of retiring before the age of forty; now she was forty-two. The company had two ballerinas each now arriving at her mature peak – Nadia Nerina and Svetlana Beriosova – and a group of excitingly talented younger ballerinas, notably

Antoinette Sibley, Lynn Seymour and Merle Park. Since *Ondine*, Ashton had choreographed only one *pas de deux* on Fonteyn. His 1960 two-act ballet *La Fille mal gardée*, for Nerina, had been the greatest success he had ever had (and a big hit in Russia). Earlier in 1961, he had made another popular two-act ballet, *The Two Pigeons*, on Lynn Seymour. A rich but non-Fonteyn phase of his career had begun. This would have been a perfect moment for Fonteyn to bow out graciously. And yet her left foot was no longer hurting. She had always revered and learnt from Russian dancers, but she had never been partnered by one. Onto the bandwagon she went.

Very possibly, the condition of Fonteyn's left foot and her sheer grit would have enabled her to prolong her career anyway. (She now resumed the role of Odette–Odile in *Swan Lake*.) She was, however, the first to acknowledge that Nureyev played a very important part. While she was rehearsing the *fouetté* turns, Nureyev asked her 'What is your mechanic for *fouetté*?' Fonteyn, who had never analysed the step verbally, simply tried the step again. Nureyev said, 'Left arm is too back.'[3] This slight correction helped her to re-master the step.

Even during *Giselle* rehearsals they began thinking of what other ballets they could dance together. After watching Fonteyn dance Odette–Odile with David Blair, Nureyev came to her dressing-room. 'It is very beautiful performance.'³ However, he felt that the mime passages, which Fonteyn had performed since 1935, would not suit him. 'I am afraid I will ruin your *Swan Lake*,' he said. Fonteyn looked him in the eye and said, 'Just you try.'³ In the event, the *Giselle* performance was a sensation. Londoners stamped and shouted; Nureyev, in genuine gratitude and emotion, sank to one knee as he kissed her hand. Film of their dancing in Act II shows, above all, how exemplary the *legato* of her dancing is, absolutely simple in its fluency.

Nureyev's temper soon became legendary and Fonteyn was occasionally its recipient. With her instinctively good manners and her sheer professionalism, she knew how to cope. One detects her stoicism in the restraint with which she writes of Nureyev: 'Among his boyish charac-teristics was an inability to say "I am sorry" and a difficulty in expressing standard social phrases like "Thank you for your help." They apparently struck him as stilted or false.'⁴ Although his worst behaviour would certainly have been alien to

Fonteyn, she simply writes, 'I learned that the secret when he snarled was to make him laugh'.[5]

One reason she endured his scathing scenes was that he gave her what any dancer most craves: new roles to dance. Or, rather, old roles reproduced with his litmus-paper-like memory from the Russian repertory he had danced and watched. Four of these items were late nineteenth-century works (or excerpts from works) by Marius Petipa – the master who had choreographed *The Sleeping Beauty* and had helped to choreograph the versions of *Giselle* and *Swan Lake* danced by Fonteyn. Three of them would become centrepieces of her repertory until 1973: the *pas de deux* from *Le Corsaire*; the Kingdom of the Shades scene from *La Bayadère*; and *Raymonda* (usually dancing only its third act, which is often performed by itself). Petipa's choreography set off, to perfection, the amplitude of her line, the *brio* and *rubato* of her musicality, and her very considerable virtuosity – indeed, the whole ballerina essence she had built up since the 1930s. And she, with her consummate knowledge of older Russian traditions and her own British restraint and lyricism, at once stamped the unfamiliar Petipa vehicles as her own.

Some maintain that the *pas de deux* from *Corsaire* was the ideal vehicle for their partnership, because it demonstrated just how different they were. He was at his most exotic, a flaring powerhouse of sensual energy; she was at her most cat-with-the-canary – poised, fragrant, sparkling. When first they danced it, in 1962, the applause lasted twice as long as the dancing. In the *Bayadère* scene that Nureyev staged for the Royal Ballet in 1963, his splendour may have been expected, but the authority and scintillation of Fonteyn's performance was a grand surprise. The new height of her jumps, the dazzling pace and control of her turns: these showed her technique on a new summit. More memorable yet was the sculptural refinement she brought to the *adagio* passages. And her way of dancing the third act of *Raymonda*, which she first danced in 1965, became, for almost all who saw it, indelible. In the great solo (a classical variation on a Hungarian *czardas*), in which she imperiously claps her hands to cue the conductor and then drifts, in exotic nostalgia, across the stage on pointe in *bourrées*, as if pulled along this path or into that whorl by the single notes played by the pianist, she was both mistress and slave of her music.

These roles were the most marvellous she had acquired for years – perhaps since *Sylvia* (1952) – and she owed them to Nureyev. Plum parts had come to her in her mid-forties: no wonder she was grateful. She was helped in her new technical command by the rigorous classes of Valentina Pereyaslavec, a Russian teacher whom Nureyev had discovered in New York. The dancer Georgina Parkinson was amazed to see Fonteyn, in her forties, submitting herself in public to this completely different method of practising ballet steps: 'in ninety degrees of New York heat, doing pliés for sixteen counts down and sixteen counts up'.[6]

Meanwhile, naturally enough, other new vehicles soon came the way of the hottest partnership in ballet. The first was by Ashton, *Marguerite and Armand* (1963), his version of the love story of the Lady of the Camelias, to music by his beloved Liszt. The ballet is sentimental, and the fact that nobody else has ever danced it indicates that it lacks the flights of pure dance that distinguish most of Ashton's finest works. Nonetheless, Fonteyn's performances of it made an extraordinary effect in the theatre; as late as 1977, scores of people would gasp out loud in sudden emotion as she revealed this or that facet of Marguerite's heart.

Later, reflecting on the Nureyev 'bandwagon' she had boarded, she wrote, 'The era of the ballerina is over'.[7] Not that there were no more ballerinas, but that they no longer predominated. She attributes this directly to Nureyev:

> He soon set about the classical ballets, determined to make the principal male role at least as important as the ballerina's. This came as something of a jolt to those of us accustomed to having most of the limelight. . . . As a natural conservative, it was a little while before I appreciated the revolution taking place around me, but I respected his intelligence and acknowledged the wisdom of turning oneself into a movable object when faced with an irresistible force – although I didn't give in without a struggle.[8]

Did the Fonteyn–Nureyev partnership have a sexual dimension off stage? Sources differ, emphatically. Fonteyn herself writes, 'Hardly anyone knew where truth ended and fantasy began.'[9] The personal affection between them was complex and enduring. But Nureyev was intrinsically homosexual: a fact which Fonteyn soon acknowledged with grace, humour and tact. Certainly the early 1960s were a problematic period in her marriage with Arias.

During 1962 the couple had sold their London house, so that Arias now spent more time in Panama. His father had died, he himself was 'profoundly at a loss for direction in his life', and he suffered an attack of shingles.[10] While he was preparing himself to plunge back into Panamanian politics, she was busy dancing. The amount of time spent with Nureyev led to scandal about them. At some point, it seems, Arias became embroiled with the wife of one of his political colleagues. It also seems that he still needed Fonteyn's money. (Merce Cunningham remembers visiting Fonteyn in New York when she was discussing with Arias the cost of his daughter's wedding arrangements. 'Well,' said Fonteyn stoically, 'I'll just have to dance one more *Swan Lake*.')[11] It has even been claimed that she began divorce proceedings.

In June 1964, while his car was waiting at a red light, Arias was shot five times by his political colleague Alfredo ('Yinyi') Jimenez. As a result, he was quadruplegic for the rest of his life. The official story, which Fonteyn upheld, was always that this shooting was politically motivated. Rumours, however, began to leak during Fonteyn's lifetime, and have since become widely published, that Arias had been conducting a prolonged and flagrant affair with Jimenez's wife and that Jimenez shot him out of jealousy.

Then and for a long time to come, Fonteyn's mind refused, she writes, 'to conceive the possibility of permanent, serious injury'.[12] She was, however, practical and committed. She and Nureyev danced the premiere of the choreographer Kenneth MacMillan's *Divertimento pas de deux*. She then flew to Panama, where the full seriousness of her husband's injury first became apparent to her. For two weeks, she watched Arias's condition improve. She arranged (against the advice of his Panamanian family) for him to be flown to Britain, where he would receive first-rate rehabilitation treatment at Stoke Mandeville Hospital; he stayed there for two years. And, since she realized that both of them now needed cash, she started to dance again.

Tenacity, the quality she so often invoked in later years, was never more evident. Nureyev's new production of the three-act *Raymonda* in Italy and Lebanon, his new production of *Swan Lake* (extensively rechoreographed) in Vienna, his new production of the *grand pas* from *Paquita* in London, her first and last Dying Swan for a TV special to honour Winston Churchill: between July and

November 1964, she tackled all these, as well as dancing roles in more familiar productions. Meanwhile, when working in London, she took the train to spend each night at Stoke Mandeville; and she took driving lessons, passed her test first time, bought a car and drove herself between Stoke Mandeville Hospital and the railway station.

During this time, Arias consistently begged her, she writes, to let him die. After talking to other patients in the hospital, she encouraged him to make no decision until his health had begun to improve. Dancing gave her something to concentrate on other than her concern for Arias's life and health; she said later that this 'kept her sane'.[13] Her cheerful good manners to her colleagues never faltered and on stage she gave transcendent performances in roles such as Chloë, where her final happiness flooded the theatre. It remains moving to contemplate how, in personal circumstances so bleak, Fonteyn achieved such joy and such purity in her dancing.

NINE

NO FAREWELL
PERFORMANCE
1965–79

Fonteyn invariably managed either to suppress
scandal or to calm it. The ballet scandal that
opened 1965 was largely suppressed at the time.
Kenneth MacMillan had created his new version of
the three-act *Romeo and Juliet* on his 'muse', the young
ballerina Lynn Seymour, and her partner Christopher
Gable – but the general public was not allowed to
know this, because, as soon as it became apparent in
rehearsals that the ballet might be a big success, the
powers at Covent Garden announced that the first-
cast performances in London and then in New York
must be danced by Fonteyn and Nureyev. The effect
on the two younger dancers was devastating.

The situation became more complicated when it
became clear in rehearsal that MacMillan's original

choreography for Juliet did not suit Fonteyn. The balcony scene *pas de deux*, the most rapturous expression of the young lovers' new emotion for each other, had some passages that Fonteyn chose simply to revise. Seymour's Juliet began gauche and was transformed by abandoned sensual passion into a creature of reckless temper and emotional violence. Fonteyn's whole conception was radically different: innocent, pure, vulnerable, poetic, refined, noble. Much has been made of this contrast, although it is more useful to observe that MacMillan gave great interpretative leeway to all his Juliets. Antoinette Sibley and Merle Park also enjoyed triumphs when they first danced the role that same season and the role has afforded pleasing material to numerous ballerinas ever since. Still, no Juliet has been further from the whole spirit of MacMillan's dance-drama than Fonteyn's.

That is on the one side. On the other is Fonteyn's huge impact in the role. She could still seem to shine with the brightness of youth; and she knew – none better – how to shape a ballet, scene by scene, and build it to a climax. The most delicate of her touches registered powerfully. In New York, the ovation for her and Nureyev at the end of the evening lasted forty minutes.

From now on, however, the Royal Ballet began to encourage Fonteyn and Nureyev to spend more time away from the company. And it is at this time that Fonteyn began to stop dancing most of her great Ashton roles. (He choreographed nothing on her between 1964 and 1975.) Ashton still thought of her performances as *hors concours*, and remained immensely fond of her. But the years were now starting to take their gentle toll on her former freshness. And he had a company brimfull of talent. *Ondine*, although other ballerinas had danced it, he simply took out of repertory; *Symphonic Variations*, *Daphnis and Chloë* and *Sylvia* he now cast with younger dancers. Fonteyn's roles in these ballets had been among her most sublime achievements; how strange to consider her career continuing without them. In 1970, the year of her fifty-first birthday, Ashton retired from the artistic direction of the Royal Ballet. At the farewell gala to mark his departure at Covent Garden, Fonteyn danced no fewer than five Ashton roles, some for the last time.

The story of her dancing between 1966 and 1976, when she gave her final performances in a three-act role, is awkward. Was the glass half full? She continued to bring deepening understanding to her roles. Was the glass half empty? Her dance powers gradually diminished. (In her 1975 *Autobiography*, she herself rattles through the last nine years in a mere chapter.) She kept up *Giselle*, *Swan Lake* and *The Sleeping Beauty* as long as she could, because she knew that they remained the ultimate challenges to her stamina; her longevity in the latter two is without equal in the history of ballet. Her youthfulness as Aurora still seemed definitive, and there were performances in which her balances in the Rose Adagio seemed more phenomenal than ever.

The cost of her continuing career to other ballerinas was severe. But New York, in particular, wanted Fonteyn and Nureyev, who led a far higher proportion of performances there than they did in London. And Fonteyn and Nureyev wanted to dance, every night if possible; if not with the main Royal Ballet, then with its touring company; if not with either Royal troupe, then elsewhere. Fonteyn also encouraged Nureyev to dance with younger ballerinas, and she in turn danced with younger men. She could still whip up excitement in a concluding passage (as in *La Bayadère*); and, especially where the steps were not hard (as in the finale of *Raymonda*), her sheer love of dancing surfaced, with intoxicating results. In 1970, she arrived in Marseilles to dance three performances of Aurora in three days.

Finding that all three performances had been sold out, she agreed to dance an additional matinee. Four Auroras in three days; she was fifty-one years old.

Particularly after 1970, she began to adjust her phrasing of steps to make her declining technique work with musical effectiveness; and many of those who had loved the consistently high standards of her dancing for twenty or thirty years found these accommodations, however slight in some cases, hard to bear. And, as her lower body began to fail, she compensated increasingly with her upper body: mainly with the use of her face, head and neck. (This disproportionately cameo emphasis on facial expressiveness – 'eyebrow dancing', it has been called – had a regrettable influence on subsequent British dancers.) In the early 1970s, many connoisseurs began to avoid Fonteyn performances; they had their memories. Nonetheless, for those seeing her for the first time, there was still a very great deal to see.

Meanwhile she spent much time with Arias. He had returned to live in Panama, but would often travel, albeit in his wheelchair, to be with her. 'He's got a marvellous brain. I feel it's rather a fair division: he thinks; I move . . .' she said in interview. 'I can't imagine many persons taking it as well as he does.'[1] The balance of power between them was curious. As the public saw, she was often there to steer the wheelchair. In Panama, when she was absent, he was visited by his former mistresses; in Europe, she had at least one secret affair. Her courtesy to him never failed. Dancers were impressed that, even at a busy reception after an important performance, Fonteyn would always find time to include Arias and to have quiet moments with him. Finding the time to do everything, and never to rush, had long been the secret of Fonteyn's life on stage; it was equally apparent off stage.

Throughout these years, people were always expecting her to retire soon. In 1970, she gave what proved to be her last performances of *Giselle*. In 1972, criticism in the London press of her performances in *Swan Lake*, *The Sleeping Beauty* and *Birthday Offering* became widespread, though some critics still found the increased wisdom of experience a more than sufficient recompense for the loss of youthful attack. Those proved to be her last *Birthday Offerings* and she danced her last complete accounts of *The Sleeping Beauty* and *Swan Lake* the next year. In 1976, she danced her last performances of MacMillan's Juliet at Covent Garden.

Fonteyn published her *Autobiography* in 1975. 'I have not concealed anything,' she wrote.[2] Not true.

Her relationship with Constant Lambert is the most gaping omission. Still, even if she had not successfully blanked it from her memory by now, she would have disclosed nothing that might embarrass Arias in any way. She also says very little about her roles. Her instinct was wholly against verbal analysis of dance, an approach she shared with her entire generation of British dancers. Nonetheless, a surprising amount of dance information emerges. Her book was, for example, the first time that any writer had pointed out how often Ashton asked his dancers to 'bend more'. There are numerous shrewd and generous character assessments, a disarming quantity of self-knowledge ('my mechanism for self-protection does not allow my mind to admit any ideas that my system is not prepared to withstand')[3] and some chunks of theatre wisdom. She wrote every word herself; and the book has many passages of real beauty – a beauty that has the simplicity and directness that people had loved in her dancing. Compared with most other ballerina autobiographies, it is a model of objectivity, self-deprecation and grace.

Fonteyn writes at the end that she wrote the book at the insistence of Imelda Marcos, First Lady of the Philippines, with whom she had stayed more than once.[4] If the worse side of the Marcos régime had penetrated through to Fonteyn's consciousness, she had, characteristically, blocked it out. On her second visit, she had taken Arias with her; it is likely that the Marcos view of politics had much in common with the Arias one. Something in Margot Fonteyn – the warm composure that overlay the steely determination – recognized its like in Imelda Marcos and saw no doubt the President's wife she herself might have been. Her 1979 book, *The Magic of Dance*, is dedicated 'To the Magic of Imelda'.

On 18 May 1979 the Royal Ballet gave 'A Tribute to Margot Fonteyn in celebration of her sixtieth birthday'. Little advance fuss was made, prices were not raised, and the audience that attended was almost entirely composed of seasoned ballet fans who understood the significance of the event. Fonteyn danced a new work made specially for the event by Ashton: *Salut d'amour à Margot Fonteyn*, to Elgar's *Salut d'amour*. No choreographer understood nostalgia better than Ashton; here he made it the subject of the work, with breathtaking results. The solo was a shimmering mini-tapestry, stitching together her Ashton 'memories': little vignettes from forty-five years of creativity. At the end,

Ashton himself entered. She looked up and saw this man, who had given her all these roles, gently approaching her. He kissed her hand, took her arm and led her off slowly towards the wings. The artist was leading his muse out of the limelight.

At the end of the performance (Fonteyn also danced Ashton's *Façade* with Helpmann; the other ballets of the evening – *Symphonic Variations* and *Birthday Offering*, danced now by younger interpreters – were Ashton–Fonteyn compositions), Princess Margaret gave Fonteyn the official title she had earned thirty years before: 'prima ballerina assoluta' to the Royal Ballet. The next day's Evening Standard ran a front-page headline: 'FONTEYN'S FAREWELL'. But no. Two weeks later, Fonteyn did a whole week of appearances in that year's Nureyev Festival at the London Coliseum. At each performance, she danced the leading Nymph in Nijinsky's *L'après-midi d'un faune*, a role new to her. On the closing Saturday (23 June), for good measure, she also danced both matinee and evening performances of *Le Spectre de la Rose*. Fonteyn never said farewell to the stage. Nonetheless, she had now given what were to be her last performances of all her major roles. After these two performances of *Spectre*, she never again danced on pointe on any stage.

'I'VE NEVER BEEN SO HAPPY'

1979–91

The mid-1970s saw a 'dance boom' on a scale that made the 'ballet boom' of the war years look small. Films such as *The Turning Point* and *Saturday Night Fever* (1977) helped to kindle yet further enthusiasm for the form. To illumine the widespread interest in the subject, Fonteyn and producer-director Patricia Foy assembled, over three years, a six-part television series, *The Magic of Dance*, screened in November and December 1979. Fonteyn's method was remarkably philosophical. Although her own career was a vivid thread running through the series, she also spoke of overall changes in the nature of ballet and popular dance, the cross-fertilization of the ballet traditions of different countries, the development of modern dance, and the vitality of historical and folk dance forms. The series enjoyed great popularity among the wider audience for which it was intended. The seriousness of Fonteyn's intention, however, is better reflected by the book that she wrote to accompany it.

In 1982, she became Chancellor of Durham University. (When offered the position, her immediate response had been, 'I must consult Tito'.)[1] As Sir Frederick Holliday, the university's former Vice-Chancellor, has observed, Fonteyn made her installation speech without notes, taking most of the academics by surprise as she 'seemingly plucked from the air of the cathedral' her 'passionately fluent' words in the cause of education. Holliday later wrote: 'She brought grace, dignity, commitment, professionalism and a sense of international presence to the many congregation ceremonies over which she officiated.'[1]

During the 1980s, Fonteyn performed a few supporting roles, such as Lady Capulet in Nureyev's version of *Romeo and Juliet* and the Queen in *The Sleeping Beauty*. She also made some star appearances: notably in Cinderella's coach, with Ashton, at the Royal Ballet's fiftieth anniversary gala in 1981, and in a specially Ashton-tailored memento of *The Sleeping*

Beauty to celebrate the centenary of the Metropolitan Opera House in New York in 1984. After the latter, her former partner Ivan Nagy came to congratulate her in her dressing-room. 'To the Queen of England!' he exclaimed as he sank onto one knee to kiss her hand. 'Panama, darling,' she replied.[2]

Panama was where she now spent more and more time. In 1984 she and Arias bought a small and remote ranch there, at La Quinta Pata; and she became a farmer, applying herself to the breeding of cattle with the absorption she had once applied to dancing her roles. There were strains: the care that Arias needed was a constant drain on her financial resources and on her own physical energy. Yet Fonteyn knew how to find immense pleasure in her life. The house, which she and Arias had had built for them, contained no photographs or dance memorabilia; electricity came from a generator; there was no telephone for a mile. She kept some dearly beloved dogs. When her friend the TV director Patricia Foy visited once, Fonteyn took her on a walk to look 'for eggs which the chickens sometimes laid in the crevices of banana trees'. To Foy on that occasion – as to other friends at other times – she said, 'I've never been so happy in my life'.[3]

The cattle had MF branded on their rumps. On a visit to London she had dinner with Maude Lloyd, whom she had known since the 1930s, and sat by the fire talking till two in the morning. When Lloyd suddenly laughed, Fonteyn asked why. 'If only your fans knew what you've been talking about for the last hour or two!', Lloyd exclaimed. For Fonteyn had been discussing cattle. She was, Lloyd has confirmed, interested in the multiple aspects of modern livestock farming, including artificial insemination and using a computer.[4]

She continued to take an interest in the world and history of dance. The pictorial/documentary book, *Pavlova: Impressions* (1984), is described as 'presented by Margot Fonteyn'. Her words of commentary show that she was interested in Pavlova's artistry, her travels and her fame, but yet more in her intelligence, her prescience, her modernity and her self-contradictions. In 1989 she retold *Swan Lake*, as a myth, in an illustrated book. Apart from the feeling with which she stresses the story's narrative sequence and its pathos, the book is noteworthy for two things: its dedication to Alicia Markova ('the most ethereal of ballerinas, my first Swan Queen, my first Giselle, my idol and my greatest inspiration' – who but Fonteyn would dedicate a book about one of her own most sublime vehicles to another ballerina?) and its postscript, in which she reflects on the duality of both Odette and Odile.[5]

In January 1988 her mother died; in August 1988 Frederick Ashton died. Meanwhile Fonteyn herself began to suffer from cancer. She kept this secret from the world, but pain, disability and fever became part of her life. She made regular and extended visits to hospital in Houston for treatment. For her seventieth birthday, she allowed Patricia Foy to bring TV cameras to film her and Arias on the farm in Panama. She was adamant that no one should know of her cancer. 'One of the reasons that I don't like to tell people I'm fond of is that they *worry* for and about me. I swear to you that I have felt no anxiety or dread or worry or anything since the doctor told me about the tumour.'[6] She then spent three days practising to conceal her limp in walking (much laughter at this once unimaginable situation) and insisted on learning her lines so that she could speak directly to cameras. Always looking elegant before the crew, and allowing them to think she had only arthritis, she accepted their invitation on the last day of filming to a party, for which she donned 'a simple little dress by Yves St Laurent' and was carefree with all the company.[6] The next day she flew back to Houston, to which she made intermittent visits for the next twenty-seven months. Nureyev, it is generally believed, paid much of her hospital costs.

In November 1989 Arias died. (One of his ex-mistresses at once committed suicide.) Fonteyn remained based in Panama, her health continuing to deteriorate. To one magazine she affirmed, 'I want my friends all over the world to know that La Quinta Pata is now more than ever the place I have chosen to live, and to die when the moment comes.'[7]

In spring 1990, although obviously in pain, she went to New York to coach dancers of American Ballet Theatre in Ashton's *Birthday Offering*. Georgina Parkinson, who knew that Fonteyn had danced only one of its seven ballerina roles, was curious to know 'how much she would remember, how much she would know. Well, she was absolutely great. . . . To practically every dancer, she talked about the music [and] about the very essence of each variation, the thing that made each variation important, the step that was the core of each variation.'[8]

The cost of her own medical bills, on top of the expense of years of care for Arias, now rendered her destitute. She had sold most of her jewellery in private, and now she allowed the Royal Opera House, Covent Garden, to hold a gala performance of MacMillan's *Romeo and Juliet* in May 1990 to raise a trust fund for her and then to provide scholarships and bursaries, in her name, for young dancers. Seat prices were astronomical; the audience included the Princess of Wales and Princess Margaret. The young French *étoile* Sylvie Guillem danced Juliet; Nureyev returned to the Royal Ballet to dance MacMillan's Mercutio for the first time. 'It was one of the most astonishing evenings I've been to, so emotionally charged,' John Tooley, former director of the Royal Opera House, who had organized the event, recalled. 'Here was Margot, far from well, but looking as always a million dollars.'[9] She took her last bows at Covent Garden. During that visit, she coached young Royal Ballet dancers, including the nascent ballerina Darcey Bussell, in *Swan Lake*. And, in her last visit to Durham University, she spoke of the importance of 'tenacity' in the face of life's setbacks.

When death came, on 21 February 1991, it was widely understood that it released her from great pain. She was cremated; her remains were buried beside Arias's grave. A tiny plaque reads simply 'Dame Margot Fonteyn Arias'; the words above both graves, at her order, were 'Nuestra Separación es Solo Geografica' ('Our Separation is Only Geographic'). It was a motto that they had long ago adopted; in her 1975 *Autobiography* she places it beneath a picture (probably taken in 1959, just before his attempted *coup*) of him greeting her at an airport with a kiss. (It is planned that the remains of both Fonteyn and Arias will be placed in the Arias family vault at a later date.) Her step-children spoke with wholehearted admiration of her saint-like nobility. On 2 July a service of thanksgiving for her life and work was held in Westminster Abbey.

The consistency of Fonteyn's dancing over the decades remains a nonpareil achievement. In this respect, she is the opposite of the 'glorious' (Fonteyn's word) American ballerina Suzanne Farrell, for whom – in her career with New York City Ballet between 1961 and 1989 – Tuesday's and Thursday's accounts of the same Balanchine ballet would often be occasions for dazzlingly different accentuations.[10] By contrast, photographs reveal that Fonteyn – even as Giselle, the role she revised the most – reproduced the same positions, with almost identical line, over thirty years. Farrell and Fonteyn are, nevertheless, alike in three signal respects. Each took responsiveness to music to the highest peaks that, in ballet, it has known in our time; each seemed incapable of unharmonious movement, however unconventional her material; each served as muse to one of the two leading classical choreographers of our century and as exemplum of his style for more than two decades. Indeed, no ballerina-choreographer collaboration has ever lasted so long as that of Fonteyn and Ashton.

Some photographs do justice to Fonteyn's dancing; few films do. Studio film tends to blur the spontaneity and musical precision of dance, hers in particular, and make too much of facial expressions that are designed for projection throughout a theatre auditorium. More revealing, if inferior in quality, are various fragments of silent film taken of her in live performance: her projection, her energy and her absorption are always engaging. Some of her style is imitable and has been imitated. Many Royal Ballet dancers were for a long time shaped by the Fonteyn mould, and aspects of her dancing are today still indirectly discernible on dancers both British and international. Her line's apparent simplicity, the strictness of her rhythm, the seeming demureness with which she committed herself to her roles: these have been been influential. Some of her style, of course, is inimitable: the lovely texture of her physical coordination, the perfect targetry of her line, the richness of her musical responsiveness, her unparalleled eloquence in stillness. What records of her dancing do survive show her as the icon of classicism that she was to her audiences. No Western dancer has done more to illumine the classical roles of the traditional Russian repertory.

Also in the year of her death, BBC-TV presented a documentary on Fonteyn, which included some previously unbroadcast material, notably her live account of the flute dance from the final scene of Ashton's *Daphnis and Chloë*.[11] This solo was long felt by many of Fonteyn's admirers to be the most wonderful of all her achievements in dance. The quintessence of both Ashton's and Fonteyn's art, it takes us deep into Fonteyn's own spirit. It uses every part of the body – hands, feet, pelvis, eyes cooperate in unusual combinations – and in it Fonteyn expresses radiance and contentment of a very complex kind. At the very moment when Chloë is restored to her lover and to her friends, she shows how deeply she is a child of nature. She dances for herself, for Daphnis, for her colleagues; she is together with them and is lost in her own world; she draws the story to its conclusion and she blithely releases herself to the music. The vocabulary, the rhythm and the current keep changing; the qualities of surprise, serenity and rapture are constant. In this little dance of pleasure, we witness one of the most profound expressions of the human spirit.

NOTES

CHAPTER ONE

1 Margot Fonteyn, *Autobiography*, W.H. Allen, 1975, p. 138.

2 Conversation with Gail Monahan, March 1997.

3 Elizabeth Frank, *Margot Fonteyn*, Chatto & Windus, 1958, p. 13.

4 Ibid., p. 14.

5 Grace Bosustow, quoted by Mrs Hookham, in Fonteyn, *A Dancer's World*, W.H. Allen, 1978, p. 56.

6 Fonteyn, *Autobiography*, p. 19.

7 Ibid., p. 16

8 Keith Money, *Fonteyn —The Making of a Legend*, Collins, 1973, p. 16.

9 Frank, *Margot Fonteyn*, p. 17.

10 Fonteyn, on *Margot Fonteyn*, BBC-TV documentary, 1989.

11 Ibid., p. 40.

CHAPTER TWO

1 Mrs Hookham in Fonteyn, *A Dancer's World*, p. 57.

2 See Fonteyn, *Autobiography*, p. 42; Frank, *Margot Fonteyn*, p. 21; Money, *Fonteyn — The Making of a Legend*, p. 20; James Monahan, *Fonteyn — A Study of the Ballerina in her Setting*, A.&.C. Black, 1957, p. 28.

3 Fonteyn, *Autobiography*, p. 42.

4 Frank, *Margot Fonteyn*, p. 25.

5 William Chappell, *Fonteyn — Impressions of a Ballerina*, Rockliff, 1951, p. 12.

6 Julie Kavanagh, *Secret Muses — The Life of Frederick Ashton*, Pantheon US, 1997, p. 180.

7 Mary Clarke, *The Sadler's Wells Ballet*, A. & C. Black, 1955, p. 108.

8 Kavanagh, *Secret Muses*, p. 176.

9 Ashton quoted in Keith Money, *The Art of Margot Fonteyn*, Dance Books, 1980.

10 Fonteyn, *Autobiography*, p. 62.

Notes

11 Fonteyn, quoted by Keith Money, *The Art of Margot Fonteyn*.

12 Fonteyn, *Autobiography*, p. 64.

CHAPTER THREE

1 Fonteyn speaking on *Margot Fonteyn*, Patricia Foy BBC-TV documentary, 1989.

2 Fonteyn, *Autobiography*, pp. 68–9

3 Ibid., pp. 69–70.

4 Andrew Motion, *The Lamberts – George, Constant & Kit*, Chatto & Windus, 1986, p. 211.

5 Margot Fonteyn, quoted in James Monahan, 'Salut d'Amour', *Ballet News*, November 1979, p. 19.

6 Ashton in conversation with Alastair Macaulay, *Dance Theatre Journal*, vol. 2, no. 3, August 1984, p. 6.

7 Fonteyn, *Autobiography*, p. 71.

CHAPTER FOUR

1 Clarke, *The Sadler's Wells Ballet*, p. 151.

2 Ibid., p. 154.

3 Fonteyn, *Autobiography*, p. 87.

4 Motion, *The Lamberts*, p. 222.

5 Fonteyn, *Autobiography*, p. 94.

6 Ibid., p. 94.

CHAPTER FIVE

1 Ashton, in conversation with Macaulay, *Dance Theatre Journal*, op. cit., p. 6.

2 Clarke, *The Sadler's Wells Ballet*, p. 203.

3 Interview with Ashton, op. cit, p. 6.

4 Sol Hurok, *The World of Ballet*, Robert Hale, 1955, p. 193.

5 Fonteyn, *Autobiography*, p. 100.

6 Ibid., p. 101.

7 Roland Petit on Madonna Benjamin, Channel 4 documentary, *Secret Lives – Margot Fonteyn*, December 1997.

8 Fonteyn, *Autobiography*, p. 101.

9 Ashton in Kavanagh, *Secret Muses*, p. 324.

Notes

10 Edwin Denby, 'New York City's Ballet', *Ballet*, August 1952, reprinted in Denby, *Dance Writings*, Dance Books, 1986, p. 428.

11 Fonteyn, *Autobiography*, p. 116

12 Moira Shearer in Barbara Newman, *Striking a Balance – Dancers Talk about Dancing*, Houghton Mifflin, 1982, pp. 97–9.

13 Fonteyn, *Autobiography*, p. 115.

CHAPTER SIX

1 Doris Hering in *Margot Fonteyn Tribute*, New York Public Library for the Performing Arts, Dance Collection, 16 May 1991.

2 Clarke, *The Sadler's Wells Ballet*, p. 241; Maria Tallchief, *American's Prima Ballerina*, Henry Holt, 1997, pp. 126–67.

3 Fonteyn, *Autobiography*, W.H. Allen, 1975, p. 122.

4 Ibid., p. 134.

5 Moira Shearer in Newman, *Striking a Balance*, 1982, p. 96.

6 Arlene Croce, *Afterimages*, A. & C. Black, 1978, p. 378.

7 Kavanagh, *Secret Muses*, p. 175

8 Ashton interviewed on BBC TV documentary, *A Real Choreographer*, September 1979.

9 Clarke, *The Sadler's Wells Ballet*, p. 265.

10 Croce, *Afterimages*, p. 421.

11 Denby, *Dance Writings*, p. 422

12 Money, *Fonteyn – The Making of a Legend*, p. 145.

CHAPTER SEVEN

1 Fonteyn, *Autobiography*, p. 141.

2 Ibid., p. 153.

3 Monica Mason in Newman, *Striking a Balance*, pp. 300–1.

4 Fonteyn, *Autobiography*, p. 155.

5 Pamela May on *Secret Lives – Margot Fonteyn*.

6 Annette Page quoted in Kavanagh, *Secret Muses*, p. 397.

7 Beryl de Zoete, 'Maggio Musicale, 1951', *Ballet*, September 1951, p. 23.

8 Clive Barnes, in *Margot Fonteyn Tribute*, New York Public Library, 1991.

9 Fonteyn, *Autobiography*, p. 206.

10 Kavanagh, *Secret Muses*, p. 413.

Notes

11 Natalia Roslavleva, 'The Royal Ballet in the USSR', *Ballet Annual* 16, A.&C. Black, 1961, p. 41.

12 Fonteyn, *Autobiography*, p. 184

13 Ibid., p. 199.

14 Colette Clark on *Secret Lives*.

15 Fonteyn, *Autobiography*, p. 209.

15 Roslavleva, 'The Royal Ballet in the USSR', p. 38.

17 Ibid., p. 145.

CHAPTER EIGHT

1 Tallchief, *America's Prima Ballerina*, p. 286.

2 Fonteyn, *Autobiography*, p. 217.

3 Ibid., p. 219.

4 Ibid., p. 220.

5 Ibid., p. 226.

6 Georgina Parkinson, in *Margot Fonteyn Tribute*.

7 Fonteyn, *The Magic of Dance*, Knopf, 1979, p. 64.

8 Ibid., p. 65.

9 Fonteyn, *Autobiography*, p. 225.

10 Ibid., p. 229.

11 Interview with Merce Cunningham, November 1996.

12 Fonteyn, *Autobiography*, p. 238.

13 Monica Mason, in *Dame Margot Fonteyn*, Meridian programme, BBC World Service, 26 February 1991.

CHAPTER NINE

1 Fonteyn, in interview with John Gruen, May 1972, in Gruen, *The Private World of Ballet*, Penguin, 1975, p. 103.

2 Fonteyn, *Autobiography*, p. 269.

3 Ibid., p. 51.

4 Ibid., p. 265.

CHAPTER TEN

1 Professor Sir Frederick Holliday, Tribute to Margot Fonteyn, *The Times*, February 1991, reproduced in *Dancing Times*, April 1991.

2 Conversation with David Vaughan and Dale Harris, 1994.

Notes

3 Patricia Foy, 'Margot Fonteyn – A Story of Courage and Dedication', *Dancing Times*, April 1991, p. 656.

4 Maude Lloyd, on 'Dame Margot Fonteyn', *Meridian* programme, BBC World Service, 26 February 1991.

5 *Swan Lake – As told by Margot Fonteyn and illustrated by Trina Schart Hyman*, Gulliver Books, Harcourt Brace Jovanovich, 1989.

6 Foy, 'Margot Fonteyn'.

7 *Hello!* magazine, 2 March 1991, pp. 59–62.

8 Georgina Parkinson, in *Margot Fonteyn Tribute*.

9 John Tooley on 'Dame Margot Fonteyn', *Meridian* programme, BBC World Service, 26 February 1991.

10 Fonteyn, *Autobiography*, 1989 edition, Hamish Hamilton, p. 272.

11 This paragraph is adapted from Macaulay's obituary tribute to Fonteyn in *Vandance* (Canada), Spring 1991. His thanks to that magazine for allowing him to re-employ this material.

BIBLIOGRAPHY

1. WRITINGS BY FONTEYN

Autobiography, London, W.H. Allen, 1975.

A Dancer's World, London, W.H. Allen, 1978.

The Magic of Dance, London, BBC, 1979.

Anna Pavlova: Impressions, presented by Margot Fonteyn, London, Weidenfeld and Nicolson, 1984.

Swan Lake – As told by Margot Fonteyn and illustrated by Trina Schart-Hyman, London, Gulliver Books, Harcourt Brace Jovanovich, 1989.

Margot Fonteyn, letter to Mary Clarke, 1989. Author's collection.

Margot Fonteyn, tribute to Frederick Ashton, quoted in *Dancing Times*, January 1989.

2. BOOKS, ARTICLES, PROGRAMMES, PANEL DISCUSSIONS ABOUT FONTEYN

Antony, Gordon. *Margot Fonteyn*, with an appreciation by Eveleigh Leith, London, Gordon Antony, 1941.

—. *Ballerina – Further Studies of Margot Fonteyn*, London & Van Thal, 1945.

—. *Margot Fonteyn, MBE*, with introduction by Ninette de Valois, London, Phoenix, 1950.

Beaumont, Cyril. *Margot Fonteyn*, C.W. Beaumont, 1948.

Bibliography

Bland, Alexander. *Fonteyn and Nureyev*, London, Orbis Publishing, 1979.

Chappell, William. *Fonteyn – Impressions of a Ballerina*, London, Rockliff, 1951.

Fisher, Hugh. *Margot Fonteyn*, London, Chatto & Windus, 1958.

Foy, Patricia. 'Margot Fonteyn – A Story of Courage and Dedication', *Dancing Times*, April 1991.

Frank, Elizabeth. *Margot Fonteyn*, London, Chatto & Windus, 1958.

Gruen, John. *The Private World of Ballet*, (interview with Fonteyn, pp. 101–8), Penguin, 1976.

Harris, Dale. 'From Snowflake to Superstar', *Ballet Review*, vol. 4, no. 5.

Holliday, Professor Sir Frederick. 'Tribute to Margot Fonteyn', *The Times*, February 1991, reproduced in *Dancing Times*, April 1991.

Monahan, James. *Fonteyn – a Study of the Ballerina in her Setting*, London, A. &. C. Black, 1957.

—. 'Salut d'amour', *Ballet News*, November 1989, pp. 17–19.

Money, Keith. *The Art of Margot Fonteyn*, London, Dance Books, 1975 edition.

—. *Fonteyn – The Making of a Legend*, London, Collins, 1973.

—. *Fonteyn and Nureyev*, 1994.

Wilson, G.B.L. 'Off Stage', *Dancing Times*, March 1980, p. 397. *Hello!* magazine, 2 March 1991, pp. 59–62.

Fonteyn and Nureyev, BBC-TV documentary 1986, with interviews and film footage of Frederick Ashton, Clement Crisp, Margot Fonteyn, Rudolf Nureyev, David Scrase, Joan Thring.

Bibliography

Margot Fonteyn, Patricia Foy BBC-TV documentary, 1989. Includes interviews with Frederick Ashton, Fonteyn, Robert Gottlieb, Robert Helpmann, Audrey King, Rudolf Nureyev.

Dame Margot Fonteyn, *Meridian* programme, BBC World Service, 26 February 1991. With contributions by Anthony Dowell, Maude Lloyd, Alastair Macaulay, Monica Mason, Jann Parry, Antoinette Sibley, Michael Somes, John Tooley.

Margot Fonteyn, TV obituary documentary, 1991.

Secret Lives – Margot Fonteyn, Channel 4 TV documentary by Madonna Benjamin, December 1997. With contributions by: Deborah de Arias, Colette Clark, John Craxton, Otilia de Koster, Brian Masters, Pamela May, Nadia Nerina, Roland Petit, Joan Thring.

Margot Fonteyn Tribute, New York Public Library, Dance Collection panel discussion, 16 May 1991, Bruno Walter Auditorium. Contributors: Francis Mason (chair), Clive Barnes, Joy Brown, Robert Gottlieb, Dale Harris, Baird Hastings, Doris Hering, Oleg Kerensky, Georgina Parkinson, Valda Setterfield, David Vaughan.

The Rise of the Royal Ballet 1931–45, Society for Dance Research Day at Royal Festival Hall, 31 July 1997. Speakers: Jean Bedells, Michael Boulton, Pauline Clayden, Leslie Edwards, Annabel Farjeon, Julia Farron, Patricia Garnett, Beth Genné, Leo Kersley, Gillian Lynne, Alastair Macaulay, Pamela May, John Percival, Phrosso Pfister, Jane Pritchard, Janet Sinclair, Wendy Toye, David Vaughan, June Vincent.

3. OTHER SOURCES

Ashton, Frederick. 'Ashton at Eighty, interview with Alastair Macaulay', *Dance Theatre Journal*, vol. 2, no 3, August 1984.

Bibliography

Austin, Richard. *Lynn Seymour – An Authorised Biography*, with a foreword by Ninette de Valois, London, Angus and Robertson, 1980.

Bland, Alexander. *Observer of the Dance, 1958–1982*, London, Dance Books, 1985.

—. *The Royal Ballet – The First Fifty Years*. London, Threshold Books, Sotheby Park Burnet, 1981.

Buckle, Richard. *The Adventures of a Ballet Critic*, London, Cresset Press, 1953.

—. *In the Wake of Diaghilev – Autobiography 2*, London, Collins, 1981.

—. *Buckle at the Ballet*, London, Dance Books, 1980.

Clarke, Mary. *The Sadler's Wells Ballet*, London, A.&C. Black, 1955.

Croce, Arlene. *Afterimages*, London, A.&C. Black, 1978.

Ninette de Valois, *Come Dance with Me: A memoir*, London, Hamish Hamilton, 1957.

—. *Step by Step*, London, W.H. Allen, 1977.

Dromgoole, Nicholas. *Sibley and Dowell*, London, Collins, 1976.

Denby, Edwin. *Dance Writings*, London, Dance Books, 1986.

Haskell, Arnold. *Balletomane's Album*, A.&C. Black, 1939.

Hurok, Solomon. *S. Hurok presents The World of Ballet*, London, Robert Hale, 1955.

Kavanagh, Julie. *Secret Muses – The Life of Frederick Ashton*, Pantheon, USA, 1997.

Knowlson, James. *Damned to Fame – The Life of Samuel Beckett*, London, Bloomsbury, 1996.

Manchester, P.W. *Vic-Wells: A Ballet Progress*, London, Gollancz, 1942.

Morley, Iris. *Soviet Ballet*, London, Collins, 1945.

Motion, Andrew. *The Lamberts — George, Constant, & Kit*, London, Chatto & Windus, 1986.

Newman, Barbara. *Striking a Balance — Dancers Talk about Dancing*, London, Elmtree Books, Houghton Mifflin, 1982. Includes interview with Moira Shearer (pp. 97–9), Monica Mason (pp. 300–1).

Shead, Richard. *Constant Lambert*, London, Simon Publications, 1973.

Stone, Pat. 'Dancing under the Bombs', parts 1–5, published in *Ballet Review*, winter 1985, vol. 12, no 4, p. 75; spring 1986, vol. 13, no. 1; summer 1985, vol. 13, no. 2; spring 1987.

Stuart, Otis. *Perpetual Motion — The Public and Private Lives of Rudolf Nureyev*, New York and London, Simon and Schuster, 1995.

Tallchief, Maria, with Larry Kaplan, *America's Prima Ballerina*, New York, Henry Holt, 1997.

Tompkinson, Constance. *Dancing Attendance*, London, Michael Joseph, 1965.

Vaughan, David. *Frederick Ashton and his Ballets*, A.&C. Black, 1977.

Watson, Peter. *Nureyev — A Biography*, London, Hodder and Stoughton, 1994.

Ballet, November 1949, contributions by George George, John Martin, Eugene Walter.

Ballet, September 1951, Beryl de Zoete, 'Maggio Musicale, 1951'.

A Real Choreographer, BBC TV documentary by John Selwyn Gilbert, on Frederick Ashton, September 1979.

POCKET BIOGRAPHIES

Beethoven
Anne Pimlott Baker

Scott of the Antarctic
Michael De-la-Noy

Alexander the Great
E.E. Rice

Sigmund Freud
Stephen Wilson

Marilyn Monroe
Sheridan Morley and
Ruth Leon

Rasputin
Harold Shukman

Jane Austen
Helen Lefroy

Mao Zedong
Delia Davin

For a copy of our complete list or details of other Sutton titles, please contact Regina Schinner at Sutton Publishing Limited, Phoenix Mill, Thrupp, Stroud, Gloucestershire, GL5 2BU